PET TRACKER

PET TRACKER

The Amazing Story of Rachel
The K-9 Pet Detective

Kat Albrecht

Pet Tracker: The Amazing Story of Rachel the K-9 Pet Detective

www.katalbrecht.com

ISBN-10 0692640894
ISBN-13 9780692640890

Cover Photo by Chris Schmidt
Cover Art by Karen Ashton Graphic Design

AUTHOR'S NOTE

While all of the incidents in this book are factual and true to the best of my recollection, some of the names of people, pets, and locations have been changed. Although there is a growing movement in the animal welfare industry to refer to "pet owners" as "animal guardians," I elected to use the traditional term in this book.

My decision to purchase a purebred puppy from a breeder took place over thirty years ago, long before the existence of rescue groups. Since then, all of my animals have been rescues or adopted shelter dogs and shelter cats. I would be doing a disservice to my favorite dog breeds if I didn't warn you that Weimaraners and bloodhounds are usually difficult dogs to own. If you can't live without a Weimaraner or bloodhound, I suggest you check your local shelter or contact a rescue group to guide you through the process of adopting one. Over the years, I've learned from all my dogs, including my little yellow mixed-breed Kody, that it isn't the color of the coat or the breed that makes a great dog—it's the heart and soul.

DEDICATION

This book is dedicated to Rachel, the dog who once lived in the shadow of my passion for bloodhounds but who God ultimately used to direct me down the path of my destiny. When I was young, I read *Where the Red Fern Grows* and prayed for a special dog of my own, one that would be worthy of being honored in a book. Thank you, Rachel, for being that dog.

TABLE OF CONTENTS

INTRODUCTION

Bloodhounds are notoriously stubborn creatures. It's one of the traits that makes them such good search dogs: Once they're on a trail, it takes something akin to an act of God to pull them off it. They're not working for the dog biscuit or the bit of beef jerky or the scratch on the ears that they'll get when they reach the end of the trail. They're working out of pure fascination with the smell that engages them. After centuries of selective breeding to bring out their amazing olfactory skills, today's bloodhounds "see" the world through their noses, and they can detect the presence of microscopic scent particles that you and I could never dream of perceiving.

My police bloodhound A.J.'s sense of smell was like a fine-tuned machine. Not only was he capable of "taking scent" on command, but A.J. had proven time and again that he could follow any scent to the ends of the earth if he wanted to—or if I wanted him to. He could work through heat, wind, rain, cold—and he was very willing, with me in tow, to traipse through all kinds of unfriendly terrain to stay on a trail. Whether we tracked a lost child or a bank robber, A.J. had led me through more poison oak than I care to remember. Over the years I had acquired a substantial number of ruined shoes, socks, pants, jackets and gloves, trying to keep up with my intrepid bloodhound.

Despite a mild-mannered personality, though, A.J. was born with wanderlust. He had a bad habit of digging under fences and running off. Technically, it wasn't a character flaw—that wanderlust was woven into A.J.'s DNA. Modern bloodhounds have been deliberately bred without much of a "homing instinct." Their fondness for roving boosts their ability to work long, unfamiliar trails without feeling fearful or anxious about getting too far from home.

A.J. wasn't the only one born with wanderlust. I developed a tendency in my spiritual walk with God to wander off like a stray. Raised in a conservative family, when I reached my twenties I gradually grew bored of church and of trying to be "good." I wanted more in life—more excitement, more passion, more fun, more adrenaline—and I allowed myself to dig under my own fences and chase after more of the things that brought me pleasure in life.

Unfortunately, the wanderlust and tendency to follow his nose that helped make A.J. a great trailing dog also made him the pet who could keep me up nights worrying about when he might decide to go exploring again. On two different occasions during our first two years together, I stepped outside my cabin just in time to see A.J. crawling out of my yard to freedom. Since I'd caught him in the act, still squirming on his belly to break free, it didn't take long to catch him and haul him home.

The first time he ever escaped, however, had been more of a close call. A.J. was only six months old at the time. I had taken him and Rachel, my Weimaraner search dog, to a training camp during a stormy weekend. In the middle of our training session, lightning struck a tree twenty yards from where I was standing. The explosion, brilliant flash, and huge clap of thunder that rocked our campsite caused A.J. to break loose and bolt into the woods.

In an unfamiliar place, in rugged terrain, and worried sick about my dog, I took a huge chance and turned to Rachel. She was my dog, too, and so technically a flight risk in her own right, but she wasn't the run-away type. I trusted Rachel to come back to me, no matter what. I let her off her lead, took a deep breath, and commanded her, "Go find A.J.!"

She took off into the massive forest and I stood there thinking that was probably the stupidest thing I'd ever done in my life.

Ten minutes later, when she came racing back to the campsite with A.J. on her heels, I decided it had been a stroke of genius. I grabbed them both in a big, muddy hug, packed up our gear, and we all went home.

It was my very first pet detective moment, though I had no idea that there were many more to come. At the time, all I knew was that I never again wanted to feel the utter, unadulterated panic that strikes when a pet goes missing.

In the years between A.J.'s bolt in the storm and the time that I decided the world might actually need a pet detective, I trained three search dogs, forged a career as a police officer, worked as a detective for two years, and investigated dozens of missing persons and criminal cases. As a result, when I began to explore my new, uncharted career, I used all the tools that had been available to me on missing persons searches to look for missing pets. My background enabled me to conduct systematic, methodical, and technically-sophisticated investigations using everything from behavioral analysis and physical evidence to amplified listening devices and DNA testing to get the job done. In a field where most searches begin and end with a "lost pet" poster and trips around the block calling the missing pet's name, I was able to help people who really had no other resources available to them. Although I wasn't the only person to ever train a dog to search for lost pets, I was the first with a law enforcement background, and the first to launch a pet detective academy.

That unique perspective seems to have paid off. In my long, strange professional journey over the past eighteen years, the organization that I founded, and the pet detectives (human and K-9) that I've trained have helped hundreds of thousands of pet owners locate their lost dogs, cats, snakes, turtles, ferrets, iguanas, and birds across North America, Europe, and Australia. What began as not much more than an "experiment" has grown into Missing Pet Partnership, a national nonprofit organization dedicated to lost pet recovery and K-9 Pet Trackers, LLC, a pet detective training academy. And as for me, the woman who began as a panic-stricken dog owner who lost her bloodhound on a camping trip, I've become a person who can't walk past a Lost Pet flyer without thinking that there has to be a better way.

Giving every lost pet a chance to get back home to the family that loves them has become my life purpose. Finding that purpose took me on an amazing journey that radically changed my life.

Chapter One
ONE SILVER PUPPY

When I was a child, my heroes were a kid named Danny and his Irish setter, Red. They were the main characters of *Big Red* and *Irish Red*, outdoor adventure books set along the Smokey Creek and amid the beech woods and brambles of a northeastern wilderness by author Jim Kjelgaard. I was raised in Fresno, California, a large industrial city surrounded by plush agricultural land. Even though the closest creek to our house was a cement-lined irrigation canal, and the only brambles I'd ever seen were in our weedy flower bed, when I read those books, it was easy to imagine that it was me living in the mountains, going on adventures, and leading my smart, loyal hunting dog through it all.

I guess those books were the place where I first found my admiration and affection for all kinds of dogs, especially hunting dogs. I was one of seven children in my family, and we always had a family mutt when I was growing up. Initially, the idea that I could have a dog of my own and train it to respond to my commands was pure fantasy. I had calendars and posters with dogs in my room, and I made a pastime of studying dog breed guides, carefully choosing the kind I would want for my own someday. In the end, it wasn't the Irish setters that I set my sights on. And it wasn't the adorable pocket-sized dogs many of my friends favored, either. It was the Weimaraners, an ancient breed, famed for its steadfast work, legendary for their distinctive looks and catlike skills.

Weimaraners are known as "gray ghosts." Tall, sleek, smart, and graceful—the ultimate dog breed as far as I'm concerned—they earned their nickname in part because of their smoky gray coats and in part because of their swift, silent work in the field. They have a reputation for being hardworking, loyal, loving pets that makes some people think the breed is almost robotically well-behaved. The photographs William Wegman has been circulating for the past thirty years of his Weimies dressed to the nines and posing for the camera have added to the perception that these dogs are docile. But the truth is they have big, independent personalities. They are nobody's pushovers. Wegman actually started taking those pictures because his dog wouldn't let him photograph anything *else*. I think maybe that insistent, self-directed part of the Weimaraners' personae is one of the reasons I've always liked them.

My first glimpse of a future working with dogs happened in 1981 when I watched a TV documentary in which a marine biologist talked about his lifelong love for sharks. The producer asked the biologist if he loved his job. The biologist said, "When I was a child, I swam in a pool and pretended I was a shark. I read shark books, watched shark movies, played with toy sharks, and went to see the sharks at SeaWorld." He ended the interview by saying, "I *love* sharks. So for me to do what you call 'work' isn't really work at all. If you ever have a chance to be paid for your passion, you'll truly be blessed."

The shark man's words stuck with me. At the time, I was trapped in a job I hated. I asked myself, "What is *my* passion and how could I be paid for it?" I knew the answer was "working with dogs" but my heart sank as reality set in. I did not have the knowledge or experience to become a paid dog trainer and I couldn't envision any other dog-related career that I'd enjoy.

I set aside the concept of being paid for my passion. However, eight years later, I read an article in *Dog World* magazine about cadaver dogs. I was hooked. I didn't actually believe that I'd ever be paid to work a cadaver dog, but the thought that I could train and use a dog to help solve law enforcement cases was intriguing. I had given the idea months of thought, and decided that training a search dog was the next step for me.

It was a rotten, cold, and rainy day when my first Weimaraner entered my life. Long before adopting dogs from shelters and rescue groups was common place, I found a local breeder who had a litter of Weimaraner puppies for sale. After running the litter through a series of temperament tests, I settled on a curious female puppy. She had a white spot on her chest which made her unqualified for show work which was just fine with me.

Within an hour of testing the puppies I was carrying her to my car in the crook of my arm. I hadn't brought a crate or even a cardboard box. I folded up the sweater that I'd left on the passenger seat and put it on my lap. As I set my new puppy carefully on the sweater, she sighed and nuzzled against me. By the time I pulled onto the highway, her eyes were closed and she was snoring with little rapid puppy breaths. I was so happy about my new dog that I could hardly sit still.

At the time I was renting a cabin on a horse ranch in Prather, a town located in the foothills northeast of Fresno. I arrived home after just over an hour's drive with my silver prize still dozing on my lap. When I let Katie, my older Australian shepherd mix, out of the cabin, she jumped up in delight to sniff the new arrival that I held in my arms. I set the groggy puppy down and watched as Katie wiggled around and greeted the newest member of our pack.

Even though I had socialized Katie and competed with her in the canine sport of flyball, Katie had always been a bit dog aggressive. However, she'd never been mean toward a puppy, and this puppy was no exception. Katie welcomed the little puppy into our family, and a bond was established immediately.

I named her Rachel. It was a girl name that I had always loved. I had hoped to one day use that name for a daughter. But since I was almost thirty, still single, and there was no husband in sight, I decided that it was time to use it. Something told me that the name I'd saved for so long would not be wasted—that Rachel was going to be a treasured, extraordinary addition to my life.

The next morning, however, all those warm, fuzzy feelings were gone. I was exhausted when my alarm went off—I'd forgotten how tiring a new, needy, up-in-the-middle-of-the-night puppy can be. But work would be waiting for me, and, as much as I hated it, it was time to go.

"You guys be good!" I hollered into the cabin as I locked the door. Katie stood forlornly in the kitchen watching me go. "You're going to leave this whiny puppy with *me?*" she seemed to ask.

"I'll be back, Katie. You keep your eye on Rachel."

There was nothing for her to do, of course. Katie was trustworthy and had earned the right to have the run of the house while I was away, but

Rachel was a long way from that point. She was snuggled in her plastic dog crate with the door ajar and set on the floor in the fenced-off kitchen. Because she would be left alone for almost ten hours, I had carpeted the linoleum floor with the Sunday edition of *The Fresno Bee*. Rachel had a soft, cuddly blanket for when she napped in the crate and plenty of toys—a squeaky cheeseburger, a rawhide chew, and a tennis ball, among others.

My drive to work was an hour-long event, plenty of time for me to get stressed out about having to report for one more miserable day at the Fresno Police Department.

When I was growing up, my dad always called me Kathy Cop, because of my fascination with all things police. "Detective Albrecht," I'd correct him when I got a little older, not realizing that this was a foreshadow of things to come. I'd always been interested in police work, ever since my older brother cast off a short-wave radio when I was a kid. I'd snapped up that radio and carried it with me everywhere—I could speak fluent police lingo and had memorized the "ten-code" by the time I was ten. When I turned fifteen I joined the Police Explorer Scouts where I routinely rode along on patrol as an observer with police officers from the Fresno P.D. But the first job I'd taken in law enforcement, before I was even twenty, was as a 9-1-1 dispatcher. Somehow, I'd stuck with it. Now, after years of fielding calls from the desperate, the belligerent, and everyone in between, it was work that I despised.

I pulled open the heavy glass doors to the station, stepped into the hallway, and walked up the blue carpeted ramp that led into the dispatch center. I hung up my coat, grabbed a cup of coffee, nodded at the radio dispatcher, who was speaking in an aggravated tone into the microphone attachment on her headset, and slumped into the chair at my computer terminal.

I knew that from the minute I opened the desk drawer and removed my headphones it was going to be misery and chaos for hours. The phone, of course, rang constantly. Handling it was all-consuming. Some of my callers were frightened, panicked, worried—almost always highly emotional. Many of them were short-tempered, aggravated, condescending, drunk, or all of the above.

Some people called for things they should have handled themselves: folks who were ticked off because a neighbor's loud music, leaves, or roaming pets, were encroaching on their space were pretty common. There were people who had misplaced their keys or forgotten where they'd parked their cars. There were parents who called, worried sick, because their teenagers had missed curfew, and there was nothing I could do for them.

And then there were the real emergencies. There were nonstop calls of car accidents, triggered burglar alarms, injured people, shots fired, fights, fires, drunk drivers, stolen vehicles, dog bites—constant, urgent problems. The only right way to handle the volume of calls we received was to prioritize them—those in which there were injuries or an imminent threat were handled first, and on from there. "Life over property" was an unspoken mantra. The incidents with injuries or in which lives were in danger took precedence over the stolen cars, burglaries, vandalism, and other crimes against property.

But that prioritization, as important as it was, led to another class of calls—those from irate citizens whose first calls hadn't yet had any response. An angry man who called in because his neighbor's dog was barking at one in the afternoon would often call back furious with us at three or four o'clock.

Whenever there was a major incident—a car accident, for example—the switchboard would light up like a Christmas tree. The other dispatchers and I would juggle the calls as fast as we could, but it was not unusual to have as many as forty calls for service waiting at once.

I took a deep breath and put on my headphones, and in a few seconds I was wrapped up in the turmoil once again. Toward the end of my shift, there was a fire at a local hospital, and I was assigned to not only answer emergency 9-1-1 calls, but also to make phone calls the radio dispatcher was too busy to make. Most of these required calling to confirm arrest warrants, tow trucks, and the like, and with the 9-1-1 lines ringing off the hook due to the fire, I briefly stopped bringing up the dispatcher requests on my computer screen to catch up on the flood of 9-1-1 calls.

A few minutes later, when I was able to get back to the list of dispatcher requests, my heart almost stopped. There was an eight-minute-old message, and it instructed me to *immediately* call the Southern Pacific Railroad and notify them an automobile was stuck on the railroad tracks. I snatched up a line to make the call, and at that moment the radio dispatcher stood up and shouted across the room at me, "DISREGARD CALLING SOUTHERN PACIFIC. A TRAIN JUST HIT THE CAR!"

Thankfully, the drunk driver had already been removed from the vehicle and no one was hurt. But the idea of making a life-and-death mistake, the thought that my actions or even my lack of action could cause such damage hung over me, just like the worries of all the hundreds of callers I spoke with nagged at me day after day. If I was helping, it certainly didn't feel like it. At its best, this job allowed me to relay a critical message to an officer or an ambulance—and then remain in my chair, at my desk, shackled to my phone, never to even hear whether my intervention had made a difference.

As I slumped into my car at the end of my shift, I felt the familiar determination, born of months—years—of dragging myself to a job I could not stand, that I had to make a change. There was no way I was destined to do *this* for the rest of my life.

In my heart, I knew I still loved police work, but my dispatching job just made me feel helpless and frustrated. I remembered the shark man's story and I began to believe that there just had to be a way I could be paid to work with dogs. I realized it was time to start moving in a new direction. I knew I could do better for myself.

"Doing better," I was sure, started with training Rachel. I countered my hateful shifts at the dispatch office by spending almost all my off-hours with my new puppy. As fast as Rachel grew, so did my love for her. She was such an adorable puppy. Rachel's most endearing obsession was how she coveted socks. As soon as I peeled the warm socks off my tired feet, Rachel would be there to pick them up with her soft, bird-dog mouth. She would waddle off, the white socks dragging between her pudgy legs. Once she entered her crate, she would cuddle and nudge the cotton blobs. She never chewed or damaged a sock—instead, she treated them like fragile baby birds. It was hard to remain crabby when, after a miserable day at work, I walked in my front door to be greeted by a wiggling, silver puppy that was excited to see my stinky feet.

I was smitten with Rachel's looks. As she grew older, I took her out in public as often as I could. My intention, at first, was to practice obedience, to socialize her to crowds of people, and to expose her to unfamiliar noises. I knew her early experiences would either make her a natural search dog or make her a challenge to train when she was older. We practiced "sit-stay's" in busy grocery store parking lots. I walked her through crowds of people and past explosive air compressor noises at a local balloon festival. I put her in a "down-stay" in the middle of an auto body shop to get her near loud "rat-tat-tat" noises.

But, truth be told, my original purpose of *training* transitioned into wanting to show off my beautiful dog. Nearly every person who saw Rachel wanted to reach out and pet her silver, velour-like coat. One day we met an elderly woman with purplish-gray hair who smiled, bent down, and stroked Rachel on the head as she exclaimed, "Oh honey, I just *love* your dog! I've been trying for years to get my hair that color!" Being around Rachel brought joy to my life. When Rachel wasn't playing with Katie, my gregarious puppy was always looking for someone else to keep her company. A gray-striped tabby kitten, owned by one of the renters on the ranch where I lived, became one of her favorite playmates. Rachel would nuzzle and nip at the kitten, who would playfully bite and bat at my dog, just enough to cause her to back up and then entice her to come back for more.

Rachel was a natural retriever, and I wanted to play up her ability as much as I could. While the rest of the puppy-owning population was shouting "Fetch!" when they threw a ball, I yelled "Search!" and made it Rachel's first word.

As I worked with my new dog, I began to think more seriously about using my knack for training to make a career change. With Rachel's potential always on my mind, I began playing scent games with her. I started by tossing sticks for her, first in open areas where she'd have no trouble bringing the right stick back, and then in increasingly hard places for her to find it. In a pile of other sticks, she had to be able to ferret out the one with my scent on it. I never even had to mark the sticks to be able to tell which was the one I had tossed, because Rachel would do that for me. In her excitement, she would chomp down on the stick, leaving dozens of tiny teeth marks in the soft bark. On nearly every occasion and without hesitation, she would fetch the stick covered with my scent.

A successful search dog has to be able to approach any kind of geography without being intimidated—including water. My cabin backed up to forty acres of hilly fields peppered with oak trees and brush. There was a large pond located at the south end of the pasture that the cattle and horses used as their source of water. It was the perfect place for me to teach my puppy how to swim.

I started by tossing a stick up to the edge of the pond. Rachel ran up, grabbed the stick, and brought it back to me. Next, I tossed the stick into the shallow edge of the water. Rachel ran up, hesitated, but then trotted in up to her belly, picked up the stick, and brought it back to me. Next, I tossed the stick out a little farther and my dog jumped with enthusiasm into the water, grabbed the stick, and brought it to my feet.

I was so pleased with our progress that I threw the stick way out into the center of the pond. Rachel went loping into the water, hopping like a rabbit and splashing everywhere. She took three leaps, and then she vanished under water. When she popped up several seconds later, she was panicked, coughing up water, and dog paddling for her life. I waded in and pulled her out, realizing I had made a mistake in rushing her into deeper water. It was a mistake she'd never let me forget. From that moment on, Rachel refused to swim. There wasn't much that she wouldn't do for me, but after that day, the edge of any body of water was where Rachel drew the line.

I had given a lot of thought to the direction Rachel's training should take once we'd covered the basics. There are countless different areas of specialization a search dog can have, including everything from tracking criminals to locating disaster victims. There are even "water search dogs" that, working from a boat and in conjunction with a dive team, use their noses to pinpoint the location of drowning victims. But my puppy's pond experience made it abundantly clear that she wanted *nothing* to do with water. Rachel wanted to be a water search dog about as much as I wanted to be a 9-1-1 dispatcher!

Cadaver dogs are trained to recognize the smell of decomposition, something dogs instinctively do anyway. These dogs had been of critical importance in working homicides, disasters, and missing person investigations. At the time, it was a brand new field of specialization.

I can't tell you why the idea of training my dog to find dead people appealed to me. In part, it was the novelty of the field—an area of specialization that was new and still being explored. That fact meant it would be more open to new handlers and dogs as well. The close tie to police work was another factor—training Rachel to be a cadaver dog would bring me closer to the police work that I had always wanted to do. But it was Rachel's behavior as she romped around the cows in the pasture behind my cabin that tipped the scales and convinced me that she would excel in cadaver work. Sadly, my beautiful dog had a stronger inclination to investigate and roll in fresh cow poop than any dog should be allowed. I figured I might as well put that "skill" to good use.

As mystified as some of my friends were that I had chosen to train my dog to find human remains, I was confident I was training Rachel in important work. Rachel's training would prove invaluable to the people we worked for in the future, and so I was determined to do everything I could to maximize her potential as a working dog.

In every aspect of her training, Rachel sailed through easily. People often ask me about how a dog can be trained to do such sophisticated search work, but it really just boils down to what motivates the dog. In Rachel's case, she was willing to do absolutely anything (well, except swimming), from the time she was just a puppy, for a few cubes of longhorn cheddar cheese, or, on extra-special occasions, a glob of Brie.

Search dogs are motivated by one of three instinctual drives: prey drive, play drive, or food drive. Prey drive is the instinct to chase. It is what motivates wolves—the ancestor of all dogs—to race after and capture their food. Prey drive is what all search-and-rescue dogs need to motivate them to chase after people who run away and hide. In most cases, dogs with a low prey drive are not suitable for search-and-rescue dog training.

Play drive is the instinct to play with other members of the pack. Playing with other puppies is one way that dogs learn social skills. Some dogs, like retrievers, respond to rewards like a game of tug-o-war or chasing after a ball. Drug dogs need a strong play drive if they are trained to chase after and eventually search for concealed marijuana-scented tennis balls.

Food drive is the instinct to eat. Some trainers do not train their dogs using food rewards, believing that dogs trained with treats are inferior working dogs. But I disagree. I have trained some dogs that will not work for food, and other dogs that will do just about anything for a treat. Rachel was one of the latter. Although she enjoyed playing fetch, Rachel clearly wanted food, not toys, games, or tree limbs, at the end of her trails.

While there were a few books available on training search dogs, my primary training came by traveling north to the San Francisco Bay area or south to Los Angeles to apprentice under and learn from experienced search dog trainers. I joined a local search-and-rescue team as well as CARDA, the California Rescue Dog Association. At least once a month Rachel and I hit the highway, traveled for four hours, and spent the day learning all we could soak in about scent and search dogs.

Before I could train Rachel to find cadaver material, I first needed to train her to find people. So we advanced from searching for tossed sticks to searching for hidden people. I would have a "victim" run away and call Rachel's name, baiting her with a treat, and hide behind a tree or in some heavy brush. (I often took turns with other dog trainers playing the victim role, so that each dog would have a chance to make a find.) Once my victim vanished from sight, I would release Rachel's collar and give her the command, "Search!" Rachel would bolt and quickly use her eyes, nose, and ears to help her locate the human who held her reward.

Once Rachel understood that she was to find the hidden person, I then trained her that her job was to *leave* that person and come back to me. This is easier than it sounds. I found that if I turned and ran away as soon as Rachel reached the victim, and if they did not give her a reward, Rachel would see me running away from her and she would whip around and tear off to chase me down. Once she reached me, I gave her the command, "Show me!" and ran back to the hidden person. As soon as we both arrived at the hidden person, I handed Rachel a hunk of cheese and praised her. She quickly learned that she would only receive a reward once she found the victim, left him or her to get me, and took me back with her to their hiding place.

When I began teaching Rachel to search for cadaver scent, I started out by exposing her to the scent of decomposition to see how she would react to it. I did this after securing permission from the Fresno County Sheriff's Office to take Rachel to a site where they had recently recovered the body of a homicide victim from a shallow grave. The detectives were long gone, but for the sensitive nose of a dog, the scent that had seeped into the ground could be expected to linger for months or even years.

I took Rachel to the crime scene, allowed her to work up to the scent, and observed her reaction. She sniffed intently and then did something I hadn't expected—she squatted and peed. Although less than elegant, urinating turned out to be Rachel's "natural alert" and what she would do instinctively whenever she picked up any decomposition scent. I then put a command word to the scent so Rachel would be able to identify similar scents in the future.

"Bones!" I said as Rachel sniffed around the turned-up soil. Each time she sniffed the soil, I gave the "Bones!" command. Now that I was armed with the knowledge of Rachel's natural alert to decomposition, I was ready to start her cadaver training in earnest.

Any cadaver dog trainer will tell you that obtaining scent material is the most difficult aspect of training a dog in this discipline. Thankfully, another search dog trainer gave me a tip that worked well for me. I supplied my dentist with a box of empty baby food jars and asked for an unusual favor. A week later, when I picked up my baby food jars, there was a newly-pulled tooth in each container. I took the jars home, pounded nail holes in the lids to make the scent more accessible to Rachel, and was set with training material for months. The hide-and-seek training games we had long played with sticks and people took a new turn when we started searching for the pulled teeth. Rachel would soon be ready for real cases.

It wasn't long until we worked our very first case. A warehouse had burned to the ground in downtown Fresno, and the fire department wasn't sure whether reports that a homeless man had perished in the fire were true. After the ashes were cool, Rachel and I responded and searched for hours. Rachel never alerted, and based on that fact and the rest of the evidence in the case, detectives eventually agreed that no one had died in the fire.

Months later, an investigator from the Fresno Police Department asked us to respond to search for evidence in a suspected homicide case. A severed foot inside of a tennis shoe had been found and a search for more evidence was needed. While Rachel didn't break the case open or locate any new physical evidence, she did give a readable cadaver alert on evidence and managed to impress the homicide detective.

Sadly, these were the only two cases that Rachel worked during her first three years in Fresno. I slowly discovered that most of the law enforcement agencies in Fresno County were not receptive to the idea of a volunteer responding to an investigation with a search dog. Most who believed in the value of working with search dogs at all preferred to work with police officers who were handlers rather than allowing civilian handlers to assist in investigations.

It was around the time of this realization that I read another book that gave me both inspiration and the clear direction that I needed. It was called *Manhunters! Hounds of the Big T* and was about a man in New York who used bloodhounds to track criminals and lost people. Beginning with that book, I learned more of the nuances of trained search dogs. Bloodhounds are trained and used to follow a scent trail, while air-scenting cadaver dogs, like Rachel, are trained to detect airborne scent particles from a stationary object. While bloodhounds can be used to follow the route that a person walked, they are limited to being used within the first week of a disappearance. Cadaver dogs can be used months, even years, after a disappearance and still provide information to an investigation.

I began to realize that if I trained both a bloodhound *and* a cadaver dog, I would have two working dogs with a full range of canine search skills. By the time I finished the book, I knew I wanted to become a police bloodhound handler. However, I still had an unanswered question. Police work is dangerous. Police officers risk their lives daily for the sake of protecting the public. Yes I wanted to work a bloodhound, but was I *really* willing to risk my life to save other people?

Thankfully, during the time I pondered this question I watched a movie that sealed my fate. It was called *Eight Seconds* and told the true story of Lane Frost, a professional bull rider who was gored and killed by a bull during a rodeo. The end of the movie showed a TV interview of Lane Frost who said something that struck a chord. I wrote it down on a note card, which remains on my refrigerator to this day. Lane said, "Don't be afraid to go after what you want to do, and what you want to be. But don't be afraid to be willing to pay the price."

I knew immediately that I *was* willing to pay the price, just like Lane Frost had paid the price for following his passion. Working as a police bloodhound handler would mean I'd be paid for my passion and would have the "shark man" career I longed for. I made the decision to put myself through the police academy, obtain a bloodhound, and become a police bloodhound handler.

It seemed perfect: a new career in law enforcement, another new puppy to train, and the credentials to get Rachel and me involved in police investigations where we could make a difference. At the end of the road, the clout of being a sworn officer would help me make the leap from an often-unwelcome civilian volunteer to a valued member of any investigative team.

In May 1991, with the encouragement of friends and family and with my confidence bolstered by my first wonderful year with Rachel, I enrolled in the police academy at Fresno City College.

Chapter Two

ONE RED HOUND

When I entered the police academy, I knew I would get a bloodhound as soon as I graduated. In fact, the opportunity to be paid to work with search dogs was my whole reason for enrolling in the first place. I was in an extended-hour academy, designed for students who already held full-time jobs. Rather than the forty-hour-a-week academy that lasted for only four months, mine was a six-month, intensive evening school. To keep up with the bills while I attended, I continued to work full time as a graveyard-shift dispatcher. Between my job, school, and care and ongoing training for my dogs, there was very little time left for anything—not even sleep.

All the recruits at the academy had cardboard placards on their desks with their names in bold letters, large enough for the instructor to read. On the front, mine said "K. Albrecht." But on the back, facing me at my desk, I had taped a picture of Rachel and me with the letters "F.B.H." in blue magic marker alongside it. "Future Bloodhound Handler." There were many evenings when I would have put my head down on that desk and taken a long, much needed nap had it not been for my goal sitting there, right in front of me in bright blue.

After three months of total exhaustion, I got a break. The police department in nearby Reedley, California, was one of the few that was hiring. Reedley was a small, fertile agricultural town located southeast of Fresno.

I interviewed in a competitive application process with thirty other recruits. The testing included an initial interview panel that consisted of a field training officer, a sergeant and a lieutenant. I was asked questions about the law, my background, my character, and my ability to use good judgment. At the end of the interview, I explained my goal: to work in law enforcement as a dog handler. Reedley had a K-9 unit, and my statement was received with positive nods. Three weeks later, I accepted the job offer. They put me on salary until I finished my training, and I was mercifully able to leave my full-time dispatcher job and focus my energy on doing well at the academy. I graduated on December 11, 1991, and under the supervision of a field training officer, I started pounding a beat the very next day.

As soon as I earned that badge, I was ready to get my long-awaited bloodhound. A few weeks after graduation, I heard there was a litter of pups in Los Gatos, a suburb of San Jose. When I called the breeder, he seemed almost surprised to have a prospective buyer on the phone, but he invited me to come and see the pups the next day.

I went to Los Gatos, but with reservations. I knew better than to run out and buy the first puppy I saw. My plan was to simply look these pups over to help me get a feel for what I was looking for—and what I was *not* looking for. And then I'd be ready to start my search for a bloodhound puppy in earnest.

As I pulled up the steep, rut-filled dirt driveway that led to the breeder's isolated home, I was greeted by the sound of bellowing howls from the older, mature bloodhounds. Bloodhounds do not bark—they practically sing. They open their mouths, shape their lips into a big Cheerio-like "O," and out comes a long, drawn-out "roooooooo, rooooooo" melody. This was the first time I had ever heard this music and it gave me goose bumps as I approached the house.

The bloodhound breeder ambled out his front door wearing a loose black T-shirt, matching black running pants, and running shoes. Although this man was not the best of breeders, he had a reputation for having great bloodhound handling skills. He shook my hand and invited me to come take a look at the puppies.

And there they were—three puppies and their mother in a giant dog pasture where horses had once roamed. The breeder had fenced in a large, dirt paddock and lined it with chicken wire so the dogs could not crawl out. There was straw mixed in the area to keep the mud to a minimum and give the dogs a soft place to sleep. There were several large plastic dog crates, wire crates, empty stainless steel dog dishes, and a large watering trough. There were no cushy dog beds, no toys, no blankets, no collars—none of the things you hope to find when you go looking at puppies. The older, baying adult hounds were segregated from the younger dogs.

The yipping puppies were jumping all over each other with the mother struggling to be the first to greet me as I approached the gate. They were four months old—all big ears and big feet, and huge compared to the seven-week-old peanut Rachel had been when I brought her home. There were two females and one male.

The little male had big, floppy, oar-shaped, chocolate-colored ears. His coat was the color of cinnamon, and he had a soft black, velour-like muzzle. He had enough saggy skin on his small frame to cover a Great Dane and little brown Bambi eyes with excessive, loose skin that hung low below them. This comical droopy-eyed, hangover look was normal for a bloodhound, but I had not yet spent a lot of time around these dogs, and I was charmed by the woe-is-me appearance it gave the dog.

The small male puppy had cowered from a dominant female puppy, but he eagerly came in my direction when I called him. Even though he was a little skittish when I reached out to pet him, it only took him a minute to decide he liked me. He slumped against my leg and sighed.

And that was pretty much all it took. A cute pair of ears and a little snuggle and all my reservations went out the window. I had wanted one of these dogs so badly, and for such a long time, that when I finally saw my opportunity to have one of my own, and he acted as though he belonged to me, I grabbed him and never looked back.

An hour after turning up that driveway, I was packing my new puppy into Rachel's wire dog crate in the back of my new pickup truck. I paused for just a minute to look at my new puppy after I had him loaded in the truck. I had just jumped at the chance to buy a four-month-old dog of questionable breeding, and I couldn't get him home fast enough. This was going to be great.

It was anything but great. I named the puppy A.J., and in as many ways as Rachel had been a perfect puppy, he was not. I should have known, of course, before I even agreed to take him. A.J., bless his heart, had spent all of his days on this planet, right up until I put him in my truck, living in a horse paddock by an isolated house in the mountains. Because of that very limited experience of the world, he was afraid of everything new he encountered.

He must have been in a car once, because he had had his shots, but he didn't seem to remember. He was terrified while getting into the crate in my truck, more terrified when I started it, a panicked wreck when it started moving, and carsick before we even got to the highway. When I arrived at home three hours later, I unloaded my trembling puppy and plopped him down in my plush back yard. A.J. didn't know what to do about grass. This was his first experience with the green stuff under his feet. When he discovered it in quantity, he was afraid to walk on it. We went through the same horrified and terrified act with each new surface A.J. discovered—first the grass, then the linoleum in the kitchen, then the carpet in my cabin.

A.J. had never spent any time inside a house either. All the new sights, smells, sounds and textures were a shock to his system. Most frightening of all, as far as he was concerned, were the two big dogs already living there. As Rachel raced up to greet the new puppy, A.J. turned around and squeezed himself headfirst into a corner.

Katie, who I figured would be jealous, made a quick assessment of the new dog's ridiculous behavior. She sniffed at A.J. with disdain, turned her back on him, and sauntered off to the couch. That night A.J. whimpered and howled in his crate, keeping us all awake. I could hear the disapproval in Katie's sighs as she shifted around in the night, trying to ignore the unhappy puppy. Rachel seemed unfazed. I could hear her lightly snoring between A.J.'s mournful howls.

The next morning, I wrestled a collar onto A.J. and snapped on a leash. I thought he was going to have a heart attack. The presence of the unfamiliar object around his neck, plus the tether to me, was more than he could stand. I carried him outside, set him down in the driveway, and encouraged him to follow me. He locked up all four of his feet and refused to move. I pleaded and tried to coax him with treats. He suddenly lunged forward and bolted until he hit the end of the lead in front of me and froze in place. Each time I tried to encourage him to move, A.J. would burst forward and shoot past me in panic and then freeze again at the end of the lead. He was confused and afraid. I was deeply dismayed.

The following day, I took A.J. to the veterinarian for a once-over. He was terrified from the moment we walked into the office. Once again, A.J.

planted his feet and refused to move. As I tried to coax him forward, he lost control of his bladder.

I called the breeder in Los Gatos and told him I wanted my money back. "I'm going to have to bring him back," I explained. "He's afraid of everything. I can't even get him to walk on a leash. He won't eat, and he's terrified of my other dogs."

"No," the breeder replied matter-of-factly. "He's the right dog for you. You just need to spend more time with him. He'll learn to trust you."

I was shocked. I had expected him to tell me when I could bring the faulty puppy back. As a remorseful buyer with what I thought was a defective purchase, I should have stood my ground. Instead, I decided to give it a little longer. Maybe A.J. did just need more time and attention. For no better reason than the fact that beyond all his fears, this puppy had a very sweet personality and was adorable in his own awkward way, I was willing to try.

Since it was obvious we were not going to be conquering any training exercise—or even basic obedience—right away, I decided to start at square one with my new dog. I left the collar on but put away the leash for a few days and gave A.J. a chance to settle in on his own terms. I did my best to ignore his fearfulness, and threw myself into trying to discover what would make this dog feel happy and secure.

It didn't take long to discover that A.J.'s greatest joy in life came in the form of having his chest rubbed. He was happy for a scratch on the head or a pat on the back, but once he discovered I might be persuaded to rub his chest, he started trying to find ways to weasel under my hand so I would do so. After a few days of getting used to his surroundings, A.J. started, ever so slightly, to relax.

And by then, I wouldn't have returned him to the breeder no matter what was wrong with him. He was *my* little buddy, reserved and neurotic or not, and he was a part of my family.

I couldn't wait to start training A.J., and I spent a lot of my time studying and preparing for the work that would come. If I could turn my fearful, gawky puppy into a well-trained, successful search dog, then I'd have an open door to work both dogs professionally. A.J. and I could get hired as a

K-9-officer team, and my law enforcement contacts would get Rachel and me more cases as well.

Bloodhounds are trained in a discipline known as "man trailing." This training technique involves teaching scent discrimination and the use of a scent article. Many other breeds, even mix breeds, have been successfully trained to trail lost people, but I wanted a dog that I could use as an investigative tool and a partner that could search for criminals.

In reading about bloodhounds I discovered that they are the only dogs whose findings are admissible as evidence in court—and for good reason. Bloodhounds are known as "man hunters" and have been used for centuries to trail criminals. The term "caught red handed" derived from the time when bloodhounds were often used to capture poachers, who were sometimes caught with the blood of their illegal work still on their hands.

According to William Syrotuck, author of *Scent and the Scenting Dog*, about one eighth of a dog's brain and more than fifty percent of his internal nose is committed to olfaction, compared to a human's olfactory lobe, which is only about the size of a stamp. And of all breeds of dog, none surpasses the bloodhound in scenting ability. While humans have an estimated five million olfactory sensory cells inside the nose; bloodhounds have over more than two hundred and twenty million. Humans get "nose fatigue"—we become accustomed to a scent, and in a short amount of time our sense of smell becomes so dull we no longer detect it. Bloodhounds, however, continue to detect a scent as long as it's present.

Bloodhounds have, over the hundreds of years of their history as a breed, been developed so specifically for their ability to track a scent that you can literally see it in their conformation: Their noses, and the corresponding area in their brains that processes olfactory information, are oversized. The part of a person's brain dedicated to decoding olfactory information is the size of a pinto bean; a bloodhound's is the length of a thumb. The deep folds of skin and the wet, slobbery jowls around a bloodhound's mouth actually help capture, moisten, and enhance scent particles. The long, obtrusive ears drag on the ground and help stir up "cold" scent particles that may have settled on the ground. Some handlers even believe the ears hinder hearing and the folds around the eyes affect a bloodhound's eyesight—leading to an even more attuned sense of smell in the dog to compensate.

In temperament, too, bloodhounds are born to be great search dogs. They are stubborn and focused. When a good trailing dog is working a scent trail, it's almost impossible to distract him. Occasionally, a bloodhound following a trail will even run into a stationary object. Like an absentminded professor, he's so focused on what's under his nose, he forgets to watch where he's going.

Training A.J. began as a very slow process. Because of his fearful nature, I had to first wait for him to get used to the idea of every new thing, and then move on to what I wanted to teach him. The harness, for example, was a very big deal to him.

Unlike the movies that often portray two bloodhounds working together as a pair or even several hounds working as a loose pack, man-trailing bloodhounds are actually worked alone, each with one handler. They are usually fitted with a leather tracking harness with straps that wrap around the front of the chest and behind the front legs. These harnesses have a large metal ring on the topside where a long lead is snapped. The dog handler holds the end of the lead as the bloodhound works the scent and pulls the handler along on the scent trail.

If allowed to run loose, bloodhounds typically ignore people and other distractions as they track a scent for miles, even if it should cross a busy highway. Other types of search-and-rescue dogs, like avalanche dogs or disaster dogs, can be worked off-lead and are easily controlled by voice commands from their handlers. But because they are so tenacious when tracking a scent trail, bloodhounds are put in a harness—primarily for their own safety.

When I first put the harness on him, A.J. looked confused and unhappy. He tried to bite at the leather straps on either side of his shoulders. When I tried to get A.J. to walk while wearing the harness, I had the same problem as when I first put a collar and leash on him: he locked his stubby legs, stiffened up, and would not budge. I had to let A.J. just *wear* the harness for a full two weeks before I could think of asking him to *work* in it.

Once A.J. became acquainted with the house, the neighborhood, the leash, the harness, and his dreaded trips in the back of the truck, I started to take him out on short games of hide-and-seek. I enlisted the help of my nieces and nephew. Jenny, Jamie, Kaitlyn and Tom ranged in age from eight to twelve at the time, and they were more than willing to bait my new bloodhound for me.

The first games were very simple. I'd snap on the harness and lead, and one of the kids would play with A.J. and then take off and hide just around the corner. A.J. would watch eagerly, and just as his playmate disappeared, I would command him to "Search!" My little hound would enthusiastically lead me to the hidden quarry.

The next step was a scent article. Every time someone ran away and hid, I would have them wave a T-shirt, rag, or something else they had wiped their scent on and drop it on the ground as they took off. Before giving the search command, I would walk A.J. up to the scent article on the ground and point at the item as I commanded, "Take scent." As A.J. was sniffing the item, I would release my hold on his collar and give the search command.

Soon, A.J. graduated to using the scent article of choice for bloodhound handlers: a sterile gauze pad. I used sterile gauze pads to collect scent because they were bacteria-free and therefore scent-free. Once A.J. was ready to work real cases, I would have to collect scent on gauze pads because touching or taking something from the person we wanted to trail could potentially disturb physical evidence. I could collect scent from something as obscure as a chair where the subject had been sitting or the steering wheel of a car he drove. This simple tool opened up unlimited possibilities in making sure A.J. could always have scent to start his searches.

A.J. quickly mastered the short runaway games as well as the concept of sniffing the scent article. His progress in training was better than I had expected. I began to lengthen the trails, added turns, and had my helpers hide in unusual places such as lying prone inside the backseat of a car or sitting high up in a tree. Within a month or so of starting to play hide-and-seek, A.J. could easily find a person who had hidden from him during one of these games—even the ones who had traveled a good distance and hidden well.

Most of the other bloodhound handlers I trained with taught their dogs to jump up and plant their front paws on the chest of the person they were tracking as a form of identification. But because of a method I had developed in training my first dog Katie (in the canine sport of flyball), I decided to create a gentler form of identification for my bloodhound. I came up with the idea to train A.J. to sit and use one paw to "push" on the leg of the person he had found. It was the same method I used to train Katie to "push" on the flyball box to release a tennis ball. "Push!" was a common command in flyball racing, but I was probably the first to add it to the repertoire of search dog commands.

(Interestingly enough, back in 1994 A.J. and I attended a police bloodhound seminar on the East Coast where I was teased by some of the seasoned bloodhound handlers for my hound's sissy, nonaggressive form of identification. The old school cops seemed to resent a bloodhound handler who came out of California—"home of the fruits, nuts, and flakes." Today, this form of identification is widely used within the bloodhound community. I recently learned that in some regions it's called, of all things, "The California Push.")

I was a big believer in loud verbal praise for my dogs. When A.J. found the person at the end of the trail, I would either sound off with loud, "Gooooood booooooy A.J." cheers or, on occasions in which he solved more difficult trails, I would sing an impromptu song that usually started with, "Hip, hip, hooray for the happy hound dog!" I did everything I could to assure that my dog learned to love his job.

Of course, we still had at least a year of advanced training ahead of us. I received this upper-level training from experienced police bloodhound handlers, most of whom were members of a bloodhound training organization called the National Police Bloodhound Association, and from a handful of expert civilian handlers in California. Once a year, I traveled to a rural camp in Grantsville, Maryland, where I attended a bloodhound seminar with other police officers. I worked A.J. on trails where the scent was several hours, even several days, old. I was assigned to a trainer and a small group of other handlers who helped put A.J. through his paces. A "trail layer" would walk into the woods and stand in one location or walk around in a small circle, leaving a heavy concentration of scent known as a "scent pool," where the scent tends to hover in the area. It was A.J.'s job to work through the large plume of scent and figure out which direction the subject went from there.

We also worked on finding a person who had walked from the woods into a business district and then waited outside a store. A.J. passed this with flying colors, ignoring passersby and honing in on his trail layer. We trained on "split trails," where two or three people walked out together and then at a designated point split apart and headed in different directions. A.J. consistently took the correct split in these trails and found and identified the right person.

After each trip, I left Maryland with a binder full of information and a head full of new training ideas. Once at home, I added new challenges to my training program. The most important of these was to teach A.J. to work a "negative trail."

"Negative trail" training means that you teach a dog to give a clear indication when there is *no* scent at the start of a trail. The purpose of working negative trails is to make sure that the handler can read the dog and know what its physical signals are when it can't find the scent. As many dog handlers have learned the hard way, if you don't train your bloodhound on negative trails, then the dog will learn to sniff the article and take off at a run, whether the scent is there or not, leading the handler on a wild goose chase.

To train on a negative trail, I would collect scent from a friend who I confirmed had not been anywhere near the area where I planned to train A.J. I would then take A.J. to the training area and present him with the scent. I knew the person's scent was nowhere in the area and I would allow A.J. to sniff around but not encourage him to go anywhere. As soon as he stopped casting about and gave some type of indication, I would praise him. With A.J., he would cast about, shake off, and turn around to make direct eye contact with me. Once he did this, we would drive to the friends' house, where I would take A.J. into the cloud of my friend's scent and tell him "Get to work!" and allow him to then quickly find his target and receive his reward.

We also trained on "vehicle trails" so that I could learn what A.J. would do when someone he was following climbed into a car and drove off. While some bloodhounds have been trained to follow the miniscule amount of scent left behind when a victim or suspect leaves an area in a car, A.J. was not one of these dogs. Once the heavy foot trail dissipated down to a scattered, light amount from a vehicle trail, A.J. would shake off as if he was out of scent.

We were off to a great start. I loved running behind my bloodhound. I loved to watch A.J. work with his nose above the ground, big ears dangling, completely focused on the task at hand. I had long since decided that the backyard breeder in Los Gatos really *was* a bit of a fortune teller—he'd certainly been right about the potential for A.J. with me. A.J. and I were an inseparable team.

To be honest, the only problem I faced in A.J.'s early training wasn't really a problem at all. It was just an issue that perplexed me. At the end of a successful search, I wanted to reward A.J. for his hard work with something more than verbal praise. Most working dogs need to know that there's a prize—whether its freeze dried liver or dog biscuits or a quick game of fetch—at the end of the scent trail. It keeps them motivated to work.

But I couldn't find anything that A.J. could get excited about after a job well done. I tried cheese, for which Rachel would have gladly done cartwheels, but A.J. wouldn't even eat it. When Rachel's favorite reward didn't work, I tried the tennis ball, which could still cause Katie, now nearly ten years old, to jump several feet in the air from a standstill if she thought we were going to play fetch. A.J. didn't care about a soggy ball either. He just sat there, triumphant at the end of the trail, looking up at me.

Sometimes A.J. would accept a dog biscuit, but it obviously didn't bring him any joy. I started experimenting with a variety of different foods and toys around the house, looking for something, anything that would motivate my dog. It really never occurred to me that he was already sufficiently motivated—after all, he was successfully doing the work he was bred to do. I was determined to see the kind of joy and enthusiasm in A.J. that I routinely saw in my other dogs when they were given a reward. I wanted him to be *happy*.

In the end, with some coaching from Rachel, A.J. did learn to get a little bit excited about receiving a chunk of cheese. But in those early months of his training, I found that, as when he was a puppy, the thing A.J. wanted most in the world from me wasn't a snack or a toy. He wanted to stand stock-still and silent, eyes half closed, nose jutted skyward, while I rubbed his bony chest. I realized that my mild-mannered bloodhound was not capable of the kind of exuberant joy I had come to expect from Rachel, but in those moments, I was confident that as I scratched his chest he was content.

My training of both Rachel and A.J. was going better than I could have ever hoped that year, but my job with the Reedley P.D. was not. I had stepped into my new job eager to work hard, to make a good impression, and to fully embrace my duties as a police officer.

My first day on the job, December 12, 1991, I arrived at work a half hour early, with polished boots and a perfectly pressed Reedley Police Department uniform. I couldn't wait to drive a squad car, to make an arrest, to do all the cop stuff in real life that I'd been learning about in the academy for six months.

Unfortunately, the tough, seasoned male officers on the Reedley police force were not nearly as enthusiastic about working with a young, female, gung-ho recruit as I was about working with them. They treated me with disdain from the beginning. When I chased a fleeing driver in my squad car—maybe a little too fast and with the sirens blaring—I was razzed for "letting him get away." When I spoke to a suspect with a certain level of camaraderie to garner a confession, my fellow officers admonished me to distance myself from suspects and victims alike. I was assigned every unpleasant task that no one else wanted to take care of—make coffee, run to the store to stock up on sugar and cream, fingerprint any and all prisoners, even prisoners arrested by other officers. My status as newcomer was the butt of jokes during briefings at the start of each shift.

One morning during our dayshift briefing, one of the older cops said, "Let's see how she does in her first donnybrook." He talked as if I wasn't even there. I had never heard the term "donnybrook" before. Because he used the word "in," I thought it sounded like something to wear—like designer cop clothing, a new line of police jackets or combat boots. I slipped into the report writing room and looked it up in the dictionary: "donnybrook: *n* 1: annual Irish event once know for its brawls 2: an uproarious brawl."

"Great," I muttered to myself. "They want to see me get my butt kicked." I eventually *did* prove myself by being the first officer to arrive at the scene of a large bar fight where I managed to single-handedly disperse the crowd—albeit by nearly running over several combative drunks with my patrol car when I came skidding into the center of the fight. I never gave a full explanation to the other officers, who arrived moments after the crowd dispersed, though. I needed all the credit I could get with them.

Although I didn't appreciate how I was treated, I was content to learn the ropes in the Reedley job. I knew I was working towards my *real* goal of using my two search dogs. And I might have been able to tolerate all of it, had it not become obvious I would never work my dogs in Reedley.

One day while I was on duty, a family called in to report that their four-year-old daughter was missing. The family lived in my neighborhood, and I was eager to help them. A.J. was kenneled at home just a block away. At the scene, officers conducted an interview with the child's parents, who were increasingly alarmed that something terrible might have happened to their little girl. I knew from what I had seen from A.J. in training that he would be a good resource for the case, and I asked the on-duty sergeant for permission to bring my bloodhound to the house and work the scene.

The Sergeant flatly said, "No."

The missing girl was found about an hour later. She had crawled underneath a table in her house, curled up, and fallen asleep. I was very relieved to find out that she was home and unharmed, but dismayed that my services had been declined.

I am often asked the question, "Why would a police department turn down an offer to use a trained bloodhound?" All I can say is that this incident was not the only time a police agency declined my offer. I have talked to many other police bloodhound handlers who've had their services rejected as well. In most cases, it seems to boil down to either skepticism about what a bloodhound can do, or resentment from someone on the force. Either way, it happens often.

The incident was one of many that left me with the certain knowledge that my job in Reedley was not what I had dragged myself through six exhausting months of police training for. I had started on this path so I could work with search dogs. I had achieved my credentials as a police officer. I had passed my one-year probation. I had acquired and trained two fantastic dogs.

My passion to work a bloodhound was evident through my constant chattering about what I was learning about training them. But the other Reedley officers were not impressed with my excitement. I was expected to be a street cop—that was the work I had been hired for. Although I had sensed a positive response toward my dog handling aspirations during my initial job interview, the actual police officers and supervisors I worked with had an entirely different view. I didn't realize it at the time, but my passion for working search dogs was viewed as arrogance. How could a rookie assume she would be awarded a coveted K-9 handler position?

The final confirmation that I needed to move on came in December 1992, after I completed my first year. There was a vacancy for a K-9 handler position in Reedley. Traditional police K-9 units consist of patrol dogs, also known among police officers as "land sharks" because they are trained to bite. Patrol dogs are highly versatile and can be used to control a crowd, search a building, locate drugs, track a scent, protect an officer, and apprehend a suspect. The problem is that the primary focus of patrol dog training is on their bite and apprehension work, not on finding people. And the methods used to train patrol dogs to track a scent did not come close to the technically advanced scent discrimination training techniques like spilt trails, aged trails, and negative trails that I had learned through the National Police Bloodhound Association.

I truly believed that adding a bloodhound to the Reedley Police K-9 unit would enhance the department. If anything, adding a cadaver dog and a bloodhound would have strengthened the police departments' chances of locating criminals, missing persons, and physical evidence. I applied for the position, but indicated that I wanted to use a bloodhound, my own bloodhound, instead of a German shepherd patrol dog. The lieutenant accepted my application and told me that he "would have to think about it." One week turned into three weeks and I still had heard nothing.

When I finally asked a superior officer if he knew the status of my application, he answered with what I had suspected for some time: "Bloodhounds have never been used here in Reedley and they never will be. If you want to work your bloodhound, then you need to go work elsewhere."

The day after my formal rejection for the dog handler position in Reedley, I sat down to work on a new "to do" list. Item number one was finding a new job. It was time to create my next opportunity.

Chapter Three
THE VOICE

It was March of 1993 when I reached my final breaking point. I knew I needed to move on from Reedley to find a job with a police department that would allow me to use my search dogs. The only problem was that I had no idea where I should go. I prayed about it because I believed in God but frankly I was unprepared for what was about to happen. My conservative upbringing and my job in law enforcement had simply *not* prepared me for a supernatural experience!

For several years the police officer part of me felt very conflicted about mentioning the incident that I'm about to share. At the time, I couldn't publically talk about what happened without damaging my career as a police officer. There was also a very real risk that I could be carted off in a straight-jacket. I'm enough of a realist today to know that many people won't believe me, however, my story would not be complete unless I share it.

At this time in early 1993, my walk with the God had been rather weak. I was raised in a religion that taught me to attend church but had lived a self-absorbed, hedonistic life where I chased after things that either made me happy or made me feel good. My lifestyle had led me to a place of independence where I didn't *need* God. Yet in that spring of 1993, I found myself deeply unhappy at my job in Reedley because my desire to use A.J. and Rachel was blocked.

I stopped drinking. I stopped sleeping around. I began attending church on a regular basis. Ever so slowly, I started to look to God for help. My heart began to soften, and at some point I asked God for forgiveness and asked Him to direct my life. This was an amazing experience and yet a difficult adjustment for me! I'd been brainwashed into thinking that it was *good* to be independent. I was shocked to learn that God wants us to be dependent on

Him, not ourselves, and that He desires to have a close, personal relationship with us.

I recalled that at some point I'd heard a sermon about how to hear God's voice. The pastor shared how God can speak to us in our thoughts, through his written word, through an audible voice, or through visions. The pastor stressed that even in our day and age, God is "the same yesterday, today, and forever" and that He is the same God who spoke to Abraham, Jesus, prophets, and the saints of the New Testament. As strange as it sounds, I was intrigued.

The pastor explained that God still speaks to His children today, if only we will believe and listen. He also warned that caution is needed because the voice, which typically is inaudible and comes in the form of thoughts, can come from three different sources; our own thoughts, thoughts from Satan designed to deceive us and pull us away from God, and thoughts from the Holy Spirit designed for our ultimate good.

During the sermon, the pastor related a story of how he was shaving in front of his mirror one day and had prayed, "Father, if there is anything that you would have me do today, please show me what that would be." Immediately God put into his thoughts four specific things that he should do that day. The pastor had said he thanked God, and then suddenly remembered a fifth thing he had already planned for that day, which he decided to do first. Just as soon as he had that thought, the pastor clearly heard a voice inside his head that said, "That was not me." The pastor shared that God showed him that if he had done that fifth project first, he never would've had time to do the four things that God wanted him to do for that day.

I was very moved by this story. I thought this type of revelation from God was limited to those who were walking closely with Him. But after hearing this sermon, I believed it was possible to hear God's voice. I knew I was a pitiful example of a Christian and felt I was the most unlikely person on the planet to have such a profound spiritual experience. But I was at a crossroad in my life. I knew I needed God's direction. In spite of my shallow, hypocritical spiritual life, I felt a desperate desire to hear God's voice.

As I began to search for other law enforcement job opportunities, a friend told me about Santa Cruz, located on the central coast of California. She told me it was a beautiful area surrounded by a redwood forest with incredible views of the Monterey Bay. I had never been to Santa Cruz, but I was interested in checking into jobs in that area. During my research, I learned that the Scotts Valley Police Department, a town located in the redwoods just ten minutes from Santa Cruz, was in the process of hiring for a police officer position. I was told that the Scotts Valley Police Department was specifically interested in hiring a female police officer.

So I called the Scotts Valley P.D. to see how I could apply for that job. Unfortunately, I was told that I had just missed the deadline by five days. I left my name and phone number and told them I would appreciate it if they would call me when they had their next opening. What complicated my attempts to find employment during this time was the fact that we were in the midst of a national recession. Many police agencies were experiencing massive budget cuts. There were very few police agencies hiring police officers, so finding a job opening was just not very likely.

The following morning, I set out to do what my dad had taught me to do when I needed to calm my nerves. I went fishing. Tears streamed down my cheeks as I cast my lure into the still waters of Lost Lake. What an appropriate name for a place to be fishing! I desperately wanted to leave Reedley, but I had no idea where to go. I cried out to God. I asked Him to direct me. In my prayer I mentioned my strong desire to work in a cool, mountain environment with my dogs.

Then I prayed the prayer that changed my life. Knowing my desperation for finding a new job and recalling my desire to hear His voice, I remembered that pastor's story and prayed, "God, if there is anything you'd have me do today, I ask that you'd speak that to me."

The idea I even believed it was possible to hear the voice of God put me in a rather awkward position. Think about it. As a police officer, I'd been paid to lock up people who claimed they'd heard voices like this! Yet something told me this was a major turning point in my life—that I had learned a spiritual truth and the ball was now in my court. The question was, *would I believe?*

Immediately after asking God to speak to me, I didn't hear a thing. Instead, I felt an instant inner knowledge that I was supposed to go to the Fresno Bible House. I had no idea if I was supposed to buy a book or if I was going to meet someone there. All that I knew was that God had placed that thought in my mind.

It is hard to describe how happy, excited, and at peace I felt at that moment. Along with knowing that God spoke to my heart, I also experienced a joyful feeling of God's presence and a peace that God knew what was best for me. I recalled a scripture (Jeremiah 29:11) that says God has a specific purpose and plan for my life and that it is a *good* plan.

I reeled in my fishing lure, packed up my gear, got into my car and started to drive home. Although the Fresno Bible House would not open for another hour, I would have enough time to shower and change clothes.

As I was driving on Herndon Avenue, I noticed a car coming from the opposite direction flashing its headlights. As the vehicle passed with a blaring horn, I recognized that it was my sister Barb's car. I pulled to the side of the road and waited as Barb turned around and pulled in behind me. She jumped out of her car and ran up to my window.

"Captain Bond from Scotts Valley P.D. just called," Barb said with excitement. "He said that if you can drive over there today and put your application in, they'll allow you to test for the police officer job."

I could not believe it. I knew they were making a special exception for me to apply for the job. It was unusual that a government agency would allow me to turn in an application five days after the deadline. I praised God for his goodness as I drove home. As soon as I walked in the door, I dialed the phone number and reached Captain Bond.

"If you can get here before four," said Captain Bond, "I can accept your application. You will also need to drive back here on Saturday to take the written test and the physical agility test."

"Not a problem," I told him with excitement in my voice, "I'm heading out the door right now. I should arrive by two o'clock."

As I hung up the phone, I rejoiced with excitement. This job opportunity was a true miracle! I had learned enough about how to recognize an open door vs. a closed door when it came to opportunities. In the past, I had pursued other job opportunities that ended with a closed door. I quickly showered and headed out the door with my resume in hand.

It was not until I was driving on Shaw Avenue, approaching Brawley Avenue, that I heard the voice. If another person had been sitting inside my car with me, I don't really know whether they would've heard it. Yet the voice was as sharp, as clear, as loud, and as real as any other voice I've heard coming from a person in my presence. The voice asked a simple question: "*Where are you going?*"

Instantly I knew that I was *not* supposed to chase after this job. Not even an hour earlier, God had spoken to my heart saying I was supposed to drive to the Fresno Bible House, not to the Scotts Valley Police Department!

The reason I immediately knew the voice I heard was not from my own mind was that it went against everything I wanted at that moment in my life. It was challenging me to turn around. To stop pursuing what I thought was the perfect job. But I didn't want to turn around—I wanted to go after that job in Scotts Valley!

I began to beg, cry, and plead with God. "Oh God, *PLEASE*. You know how much I hate my job and how much I want this job in Scotts Valley. You know I want to live in the mountains and how trapped I feel here. If there is *any way* I can get this job, please let me have it."

But rather than feeling like I was released to continue driving, God began to show me things that confirmed that I was not to pursue that job. He reminded me of a sermon where I had learned some principles of discerning God's Will. One of the elements mentioned was that God would never have you do something that would conflict with His word. If you are trying to discern whether something is God's Will or not, it would not be His will if it falls out of line with what the Bible says.

Then I remembered that Captain Bond had told me I'd need to return to Scotts Valley on Saturday to take the written and physical agility tests. But I was scheduled to work at Reedley P.D. that Saturday, and their policy was that you had to request a day off at least two weeks in advance. Thus, in order for me to pursue the job in Scotts Valley, I'd have to lie to my employer and call in "sick" on Saturday in order to complete the required testing. My heart sank. God would never bless something birthed out of a lie. This particular job was *not* a part of God's plan for my life. However, I still wasn't willing to let go.

I continued to drive towards Scotts Valley. As I drove on Highway 152 towards Scotts Valley, I continued to pray. In my mind, I still thought it would be the perfect job. The climate was perfect, it was a beautiful area, it was only three hours from family, and the money was great. Why wouldn't God want me to work there? I decided that before going to the Scotts Valley

Police Department, I'd stop off in Los Gatos at the breeder's house where I'd picked up A.J. as a puppy. That breeder was familiar with the police agencies in the area. I prayed, "God, I just need another sign that I'm not supposed to pursue this job." As if hearing a voice from heaven was not enough, I wanted even *more* confirmation!

At 12:30 p.m. I arrived at the bloodhound breeder's house.

"What are you doing here?" he asked when I stepped out of my truck.

"I'm on my way to apply for the Scotts Valley Police Department," I said.

"Why would you want to work *there*?" he asked.

The breeder proceeded to tell me that the Scotts Valley Police Department did not have many female officers, did not have a K9 unit, and that they probably would not support the use of my bloodhound. It turns out that the breeder had a buddy who previously worked for the Scotts Valley PD and wanted to use his patrol K9, but ran into politics similar to what I'd experienced at Reedley PD.

This was the final confirmation I was looking for. I called Captain Bond and told him that I would not be coming to Scotts Valley after all. I visited with the breeder for a while longer and then turned around and headed for home. In spite of the angst and turmoil I'd experienced while working in Reedley, I felt peace about my decision.

It took a lot of faith for me to pass up that job opportunity and to trust that God had a better plan for me. But He truly did—an incredible plan that would take me and my animals to amazing places. It was a plan that would ultimately change my selfish heart into one that desired to help other people and animals, far beyond anything I ever hoped for or imagined. Because I chose to believe God on that day, my life was never the same again!

CHAPTER FOUR
THE BEST OF BOTH WORLDS

There are only one hundred and eighty miles between Fresno and Santa Cruz, but in their character and in their appearance, they couldn't be farther apart. Fresno is flat for miles; Santa Cruz is a striking juncture of beach and mountains. Fresno is surrounded by endless acres of vineyards and orchards full of crops that will eventually be shipped all over the country; the area around Santa Cruz is distinguished by towering redwood forests. Fresno is a conservative, agricultural city; Santa Cruz is a funky, liberal college town.

It was a hot July morning in 1993 when I pulled up roots and left Fresno County, which had been my home most of my life. As I crossed the Santa Cruz Mountains in a rented moving van and descended toward the coast, the sunny areas in the valley and the beaches were blanketed with a carpet of ice plant and beautiful pink, yellow, and purple flowers. Just a few miles away, the mountains were rich with vegetation and wildlife. The heavily forested areas were shady and cool, the ground covered with dark green ivy that snaked its way from the ground up to the topmost branches of the massive redwood trees. The redwoods, standing over three hundred feet tall, were breathtaking. They had a reddish-brown, soft, flaky bark that was patterned with deep grooves running from the base to the top of each tree. Fernlike leaves grew out of the branches high above the ground. I couldn't wait to start my new life.

The first thing Santa Cruz had to offer was a new job. Six weeks to the day after my supernatural experience (of hearing God's voice) I accepted a position with the campus police department at the University of California at Santa Cruz (UCSC). My job there would be the same as that of a municipal cop but within the jurisdiction of the large campus. There were some differences in campus police work and municipal work, mostly in the nature of the majority of crimes. The UCSC campus, like most, had to deal frequently with issues of drug possession and public intoxication, brawls, burglaries, and petty theft. While serious and violent crimes are part of the mix for any police department, they represented a mercifully small portion of what we dealt with at the university.

Amazingly, the job at UCSC P.D. provided me with better benefits, a better salary, a department with a Chief of Police who ultimately granted me K-9 handler status, and doors that opened for me to use Rachel and A.J. on cases.

Even more amazing was where I ended up living. After turning around and driving home from the job opportunity with the Scotts Valley Police Department, it was deep within the redwoods in Scotts Valley where I rented a small cabin. Since I'd always lived in the hot, flat, urban areas in and around Fresno, this in itself seemed like a pretty big accomplishment. Bringing my things to a cabin in that monumental mountain forest made me feel hopeful and eager to build my career there. The fact that among my "things" were three dogs, two just on the cusp of their careers in search work, made it all the more thrilling. Whatever this beautiful place had to offer to us, we were up for the challenge.

There were eighteen officers based at UCSC, and they all welcomed me with open arms right from my first interview. My experience with this department was so completely different from what I experienced in Reedley that I jumped at the opportunity to take the job, even though initially there was no promise that I would be able to use my dogs on the force. Jan Tepper, the chief of police for UCSC, had promised only that she would keep an open mind about developing a search dog program. So even though I risked working for another police agency that might eventually refuse to let me work my dogs, I was willing to take the chance. All I had to do was step outside my cabin and gaze up into the canopy of the redwood trees and I was convinced that my move to Santa Cruz was worth it.

At the very least, I knew Rachel and A.J. would have more opportunities to work here than they'd had in Reedley. There were active search-and-rescue groups in the nearby San Francisco Bay Area, and we would join them as volunteers, regardless of whether I could do K-9 search work on the clock for a police department.

One of my first orders of business in Santa Cruz was to make contact with these organizations to become a member. Then I set about learning how to keep up my dogs' training in our new surroundings.

The biggest difference between training search dogs in Fresno and training them in Santa Cruz was the weather. For the most part, Santa Cruz was foggy and cool, even during the summer months. The moisture within the deep, forested areas would hydrate the scent particles, making it easier for my dogs to work. In Fresno, the weather, especially in the summertime, was like living in an oven. In the later part of the summer, it would often be eighty degrees at the crack of dawn and it was not uncommon to have temperatures above one hundred degrees for several weeks in a row.

But what really set Santa Cruz apart from Fresno was the wildlife that we encountered. In Fresno, we only occasionally came across a jack rabbit that would leap from nowhere, nearly causing me to fumble for my gun, Barney Fife-style, in my frantic reaction to the surprise. The vanishing bunny would usually be two hundred yards away, bounding off into the sunset, before I figured out just why Rachel was wiggling her tail in excitement. But in Santa Cruz, there were deer, skunk, raccoons, squirrels, slow-moving bunnies, and even slower moving opossums. The abundance of wildlife forced me to learn the skill of reading Rachel and A.J.'s body language to discern when they were on human scent and when they diverted off onto animal scent. At the time, I had no idea just how critical learning this skill would prove to be.

It didn't take long for us to get called for our first search, a sad and unforgettable one. Three months after moving to Santa Cruz, through my affiliation with the Santa Cruz Sheriff's search-and-rescue team, Rachel and I helped search for Polly Klaas, a missing girl from Petaluma. The Klaas case made national headlines because of the brazen way in which the kidnapping occurred. The twelve-year-old girl had been abducted at knifepoint from her own home while her mother slept in the next room. Police had a tip that Polly might have been brought to an area in Santa Rosa.

The search was unlike anything I had done with my dogs before, not because we were searching for a missing person, but because there were more than two hundred and fifty other searchers working the same area. Both ground searchers and dog handlers had come from all over California to try to help find this missing child. We were as diverse a group as you could imagine: K-9 handlers who were police officers in uniform, search-and-rescue dog handlers who looked like soccer moms out walking the family dog, young ground searchers who were Explorer Scouts trained to conduct searches. The mix of just the one team I was a part of included high school kids, homemakers, two mechanics, a school teacher, a security guard, a nurse, and me, a full-time cop. As a group, I suspect the only traits we shared were our interest in searching for lost people and our profound sympathy for the Klaas family.

The command post and staging area were set up at a police academy situated just a mile from the search area. We were divided into teams and assigned areas to investigate. It was clear from the hushed tone of conversations and the tense, attentive attitude of the searchers that every person there was mindful of the terrible circumstances that had brought us together. We were all hoping that the result of our efforts might help bring a little bit of peace to the missing child's parents.

Our group was told to grid-search an area adjacent to a nearby road. We searched parallel to the roadway, at times working through thick, thorny berry vines. My teammates, about twenty of them, lined up shoulder-to-shoulder and began to slowly move forward with their eyes focused on the ground in search of evidence. They were all trained in how to conduct a proper grid search.

Rachel and I worked about twenty yards in front of the team. This enabled her to detect any suspicious scent without interference from the scent of the teammates behind us. Rachel was searching for the odor of decomposition; the grid searchers for other physical evidence like rope, duct tape, or beer cans where all human scent had long since evaporated. There were other cadaver dogs used on the search that day, but they were all deployed in different areas.

I marveled at how meticulously my teammates searched the assigned area. In spite of the thick terrain, everyone plowed slowly through the painful thorns and made sure they checked every suspicious item. Every glass bottle, every piece of trash, and every item that was foreign to the terrain was pointed out to the FBI agent who followed us at a distance.

I wanted my dog to find something that would help solve this investigation. Polly's body had not been found, though investigators had good reason to believe she was no longer alive. The area we searched was where their primary suspect's car became stuck in a ditch just hours after Polly was abducted. We knew that Polly had been in the woods we were searching—and that it was possible she was buried there. I wanted my dog to succeed, and I wanted to help. I also knew that finding a child's body on that search would have destroyed me.

In the end, it was a nonissue, because the only item that Rachel located that day was a bone, one that the FBI later determined belonged to a deer.

After nearly seven hours, my group had completely covered our assigned area, and headed back to the base camp that had been put together to host the searchers. The search coordinator had arranged a dinner in the academy auditorium for the teams, and there were dorms for us to sleep in that night. After dinner, our group retired to the dorms where we were housed. As a few team members played Ping-Pong, the rest of us began to plan our strategy for how we would search the following day. We were discussing our plans when I heard a shout come from the area of a nearby television.

"They're getting ready to make a statement," one of my teammates, Ron Spurgeon, yelled. I quickly joined the group gathering around the television. Dennis DeWitt, chief of the Petaluma Police Department, was giving a live interview to the media.

"I am here tonight to tell you," Chief DeWitt announced, "that Polly Klaas is dead." That day, Richard Allen Davis, the suspect whose trail we had investigated, had confessed to murdering the young girl and had led investigators to her body.

Like most others acquainted with the case, I had suspected that Polly was already dead. The majority of child abduction cases like this end up with either no closure or a very sad ending. But in this case, we all had clung to the slightest shred of hope that Polly would be found alive. I slipped into my dorm room and wept. I had hoped and prayed for safety for this little girl. Learning of Polly's murder was a sobering reminder that sometimes our job would come down to no more or less than confirming the worst fears of the people we were there to help. It was a lesson I was destined to learn over and over in my career.

Another three months passed while I settled into my job at the U.C. campus, and then an unexpected request came my way from the local police department. As far as I knew, the police detectives in the area didn't even know that Rachel, A.J., and I existed. So it came as a surprise when Detective Butch Baker from the Santa Cruz Police Department called me and said he wanted Rachel and me to assist in a homicide investigation.

A couple hiking through a Santa Cruz park had discovered the decomposing body of a woman. Detectives and a forensic anthropologist had already recovered most of the remains, except for the woman's teeth. Without them, they could not make a positive identification. Detective Baker asked if I could bring Rachel the following morning. I agreed to meet him at the park entrance at ten.

Pogonip Park bordered the east side of the UCSC campus. It consisted of dense redwood forest, a few meadows, and an illegal but well-known bike trail called Suicide Hill—a steep trail that only experienced riders dared to climb up or slide down. Biking Suicide Hill was forbidden because it cut a deep scar into the sensitive redwood forest floor. Bike riders who accidentally ventured off the trail could end up damaging ferns or redwood seedlings, and in Santa Cruz, damaging the environment was an intolerable offense.

The weather the following morning was typical for February on the coast. The sky was a dreary gray with a low fog that smothered the coastal mountains. For a week prior to this search, the area had been drenched with four inches of rain. The moisture that covered the area made the conditions perfect for working a search dog. While the tiniest scent particles are picked up and carried by the wind, heavier particles fall to the ground and become ground scent that dogs can follow. When scent particles land on a moist surface, they stick like epoxy. The cool temperature would also mean Rachel could work longer without becoming exhausted.

The dirt road leading to the park was a sloppy mess of mud and potholes. As I drew close to the entrance, I could see the Santa Cruz City Park ranger's Bronco and a white police Blazer that belonged to Santa Cruz homicide detectives Baker and his partner, Detective Kevin Vogel. They were the two investigators assigned to the case. Two local television stations, KSBW and KCCN, also had news crews on hand to film the event.

I parked and found Detective Baker, who introduced me to the others. He then briefed us on the location of the body, the route we would travel, and the equipment we would need. I went back to my truck, prepared my search pack, unloaded Rachel, and harnessed her in her bright orange search dog vest. I waited for her to empty her bladder. In order to avoid mixed signals, I always made sure she started a search on "empty." If she peed, I wanted to be sure it was because she was working and not because she was taking a break.

Over the first year of our training, I had discovered that Rachel had a second natural alert. In situations where there were large concentrations of decomposition, she would drop and roll around on her back, just like she used to do with the fresh cow poop when she was a puppy. Of course, the most reliable alert was still the one I had taught her early on. If she found an object she believed was what I wanted her to find, she would run back and jump up on me, then return to the object and paw the ground.

Detective Vogel, the reporters, Rachel, and I descended the steep trail behind Detective Baker. The trail meandered through a flat, forested area and into a small clearing. The clearing became our staging area and we set our gear down in the wet weeds. The two cameramen primed their cameras and began filming what we all presumed was the scene of the crime.

I surveyed the area. Everything around us was damp, some areas nearly flooded. The wind was blowing and swirling and shifting inconsistently in all four directions. Having a strong wind to carry and disperse the scent would make detection of airborne scent particles easy for Rachel. It would also enable Rachel to detect the decomposition scent from a distance, permitting us to cover a larger area. Under a large oak tree at the edge of the clearing sat a large mound of excavated dirt. Every particle of dirt had been meticulously sifted for bone fragments, hair fibers, and other physical evidence. Yellow crime scene tape was strewn about the ground. The fact that the tape had been ripped down was an indication that this was no longer considered a secure crime scene. I was free to work Rachel wherever I needed to.

I glanced down and noticed that Rachel's nostrils were quivering. Though it was not perceivable to a human nose, she was already picking up the airborne odor of decomposition. She was ready to work. Detective Baker was talking to one of the reporters about the crime scene.

"The grave where the body was buried is over there," Detective Baker said as he pointed to an area out of view. "The body was discovered by hikers down on a trail over there," he said, indicating the opposite direction. "We believe we have recovered everything that can be found, but without the teeth, we're having a hard time making an identification."

While Detective Baker was still briefing the reporter, Rachel pulled me over to the large mound of excavated dirt. She sniffed the soil, and then squatted and peed.

"Did this dirt come from the grave?" I interrupted.

"Yes," Detective Vogel said, "that pile was excavated from the grave."

"Good girl," I said to Rachel. She had given a decomposition alert, and she was right. Since I could see that Rachel was already investigating, I did not want to stop or discourage her. As she began to move about and check the area, I described what she was doing for the interested bystanders. Detective Baker terminated his interview with the reporter, and the cameras turned to focus on Rachel.

It only took her a few moments to pinpoint the spot on the dirt trail where the body had been discovered by the hikers. When she found it, Rachel dropped to the ground and began to roll. "Was the body right here?" I asked as I looked back at Detective Baker.

"That's *exactly* where the body was," he said, clearly surprised at Rachel's accuracy. "I don't believe this."

One of the mysteries of this case was the question of how the woman's body had been transported from the grave site over to the hiking trail, a distance of about thirty yards. Rachel solved that mystery. From the location on the trail where the body had rested, Rachel began to move west back toward the grave. She sniffed along the ground through a brush-filled area that had not been searched. Every few feet as she stopped to sniff the earth, she would squat and pee. I noticed that several of the areas Rachel sniffed were spots where weeds were matted down or dirt was displaced, as if something heavy had been dragged. Every time Rachel peed, I dropped a piece of bright pink flagging tape to mark her alert.

When we arrived at the grave and looked back, a trail of pink flagging tape revealed a clearly defined route. It appeared that a large predator, perhaps a mountain lion, had dragged the woman's body from the grave down to the hiking trail. Rachel had helped answer a critical question for the investigators.

We worked to an area just north of the gravesite and Rachel suddenly lifted her nose. Picking up an airborne scent, she pulled me forward and up an embankment into a large pile of thick brush. I followed behind her, wondering what she was after. Rachel sniffed intently at something that was nestled down within the brush. She did not pee. Instead, she turned around, came back, and jumped up on me.

"Show me," I commanded with skepticism. Even though jumping up on me was Rachel's trained alert, I knew my dog. Rachel also sometimes used this method to take me to something that she wanted. Although she was only *supposed* to alert on evidence, Rachel often took me to bunnies, skunks, and other small furry animals that caught her eye (or nose). She had an unfortunate habit of wanting to find critters more than she wanted to find evidence!

Rachel climbed back into the heavy brush to the spot where she had alerted. Judging by the thick pile of brush, I expected she'd found a mouse.

"Where?" I asked her. Rachel stuck her nose back down into the bush. I couldn't see anything.

"Wheeerreee?" I asked again with more emphasis. Rachel began pawing and whining at the spot in frustration. I held onto her collar as I looked where she had been pawing. There, concealed within the thick vegetation, was a portion of a jawbone, with teeth in it.

"There it is," I yelled back to the detective.

"What?" Detective Baker asked.

"Teeth," I said.

There I stood in the middle of a large patch of poison oak cruelly disguised as harmless twigs, my emotions torn between the gravity of Rachel's find and my pride in her accurate work. I wanted to shout and praise my dog with enthusiasm as I normally did in training, but it was not appropriate in that setting. Instead, I looked into Rachel's sparkling, amber eyes and scratched her behind the ears. I cooed to her and told her what a noble search dog she was. She groaned happily. Rachel knew I was pleased.

The detectives were floored. They had believed there was nothing left to find, and Rachel had waltzed into their crime scene and pinpointed the one piece of evidence they absolutely had to locate to start solving this case.

As we prepared to leave, Detective Baker came up to me. "Thank you," he said. "Thank you again for your help," he said as we shook hands. It felt good to be accepted as a colleague—something that was still foreign to me since my move from Reedley.

"I'm glad we were asked."

"Your dog is amazing," Detective Baker said admiringly. "To be honest, we never expected her to find a thing today."

I stared back at him, confused. "Then why did you ask us to come?"

"I just figured that having a K-9 here would encourage the media to come out and give us the TV coverage we need to help identify this woman," Detective Baker said. "I've yet to see a police dog around here that could find a simple hole in the ground," he added. "But your dog has made a believer out of me."

That night, I watched the two news channels that had filmed Rachel's find. The newscast began with a hook designed to peak viewer interest: "New evidence in a homicide investigation was discovered today, with the help of a dog."

Rachel had turned a media event into a real evidence-recovery operation—and thus, inadvertently, made it even more of a media event. My emotions were overwhelming, as I sat in my cabin, among the redwoods, watching my dog and me on the news. Pride, pleasure, grief, and relief competed inside me. There I was, a uniformed police officer, working my search dog, on a case where we had truly made a difference. Everything I had done to pursue my passions thus far, even the eighteen months I spent in Reedley, had been worth it. Rachel's work on this case helped to launch my career as a K-9 handler.

The media called it the "Pogonip Jane Case" and it remains unsolved to this day. However, a part of the mystery was ultimately solved nineteen years later. In 2013, the victim was positively identified through DNA testing, shortly after the day Detective Butch Baker was tragically shot and killed in the line of duty.

In the wake of the Pogonip case, I found that I had the full support of my department to pursue K-9 cases. We agreed that I would continue to be responsible for the care, feeding, and veterinary care of my dogs, but the department would pay me to respond on-duty to cases where A.J. and Rachel might be of help.

Just two and a half months after the Pogonip find, an Alzheimer's patient became lost near his home in Watsonville, a town located thirty minutes from the university. The elderly man had been missing for four hours when I arrived on the scene with A.J., and within fifteen minutes, A.J. had trailed the man to a spot deep in the woods behind his home. This was our first local search with the Santa Cruz Sheriff's Office and it made a believer out of both the deputies and the command staff who were on the call.

Six months later, A.J. found a missing hiker who had become disoriented and ended up trapped down a canyon. In that case, A.J. picked up the scent trail, located the man's shoe tracks, and led us to within calling range of the exhausted man. And in yet another case, A.J. trailed a suicidal man who had overdosed on sleeping pills, hiked out into the woods, and shot himself with a pellet gun. After local patrol dogs had been unable to find the man, A.J. and another search-and-rescue dog, my good friend Jeanne Mason's golden retriever Kea, found the man near death, but because of prompt medical attention, he survived.

Later that year, A.J. earned the National Police Bloodhound Association's Lifesaving Award for that unforgettable search. His outstanding record in tracking both missing persons and criminals even earned us a spot on the Santa Cruz Sheriff Department's S.W.A.T. team, a tremendous honor for both of us.

The work of my two search dogs gradually opened doors for me and was more than I could have hoped for. By the end of my first year in Santa Cruz, I had two certified dogs and a police department that supported my desire to work them. My business cards confirmed how far I had come from the eager police recruit with "F.B.H." for "Future Bloodhound Handler" scribbled on the back of my ID card to keep me motivated and awake at the police academy. Now I carried a pocketful of professional business cards, all inscribed with a gold foil police badge and blue lettering that read: *Kathy "Kat" Albrecht, Police Officer, Bloodhound Handler.*

I had arrived.

Chapter Five
MAN HUNTER

Not long after my initial successes with Rachel and A.J., I was dealt an emotional blow. I lost my sweet thirteen-year-old Katie to cancer. Although she was the only nonworking dog in the house, Katie had occupied a special place in my heart. She had taught me how to train dogs and her death left a big empty space in my life where her companionship had always been.

After months of living with that void, I felt like my two-dog household was ready to take on a puppy. By this time, my passion for working A.J. was intense enough that I knew I wanted to train a second bloodhound. Through some friends in Maryland, I obtained a four-month-old wrinkly bloodhound puppy that I named Chase. She was a "red" female with four white, speckled paws and a splash of white on her chest that was a little larger than Rachel's was. Technically, her color was called "liver" because she had amber-colored eyes and the pigments around her eyes, lips, and nose were pink instead of black, but I would never have described her appearance as "liver" because it sounded so resoundingly unattractive—something my adorable puppy was not.

During her early training, Chase showed an intense desire to hunt. Even though she was just a rookie and wouldn't be ready to work cases for at least a year, she showed ample promise as a trailing dog. Whereas A.J. was a sissy and was hesitant to walk through prickly, spiny berry vines, Chase would blaze a trail at a gallop, crashing through undergrowth as if nothing could stop her. She would naturally work with her nose deep and low to the ground, something that actually looked impressive but didn't mean all that much when it came to working a trailing dog. Chase didn't really care about other people. Instead, she loved to receive praise and cheese from me and would do anything to please me. Anyone else could walk into a room, but when I did, Chase pined for my attention. My plan was to eventually use her on the more dangerous S.W.A.T.-team-type searches primarily because A.J. panicked when he heard gunfire.

Thankfully, gunfire wasn't an issue on the day that A.J. proved himself as an effective crime-fighting tool. The Scotts Valley Police Department called me looking for a dog that could track. The officer on the phone said they had lost a burglary suspect in a patch of forest, but they believed he was still there. I knew that A.J. would be perfect for the job—he'd already proven his trailing mettle several times on hunts for missing persons. I loaded him in my truck and hurried to the crime scene to help. Though he could still act like a big goofball when he wanted to, A.J. had grown into a composed, confident dog in our five years of training. Sitting in the back of the truck, calmly surveying the passing neighborhoods as we headed out on our search, the only resemblance he bore to the terrified, carsick puppy he had once been were those still-irresistible chocolate-brown ears and solemn eyes.

Several expensive homes under construction had been burglarized and vandalized overnight on South Navarra Drive in Scotts Valley. The suspect had been seen running into the woods. Officers had set up a perimeter, a contained area from which they felt their suspect would not be able to escape, and had that area surrounded.

Because of the urgency of the call, I took my own truck directly to the crime scene rather than going out of my way to pick up a patrol car. When I arrived at the scene, several squad cars were parked on the side of the road. I drove up to two uniformed officers who were standing in the roadway. One of them gave me an irritated look of disapproval. He probably thought I was a nosy neighbor poised to ask what all the police action was about.

"I'm Officer Albrecht from UCSC PD," I said. "I was asked to respond with my bloodhound."

The officer replied with warmth and recognition. "You need to talk to the sergeant," he explained. "Go to the next intersection and you'll find him there."

I drove to where the sergeant and two more uniformed officers were standing in an intersection, holding the south edge of the perimeter. The sergeant welcomed me and said he was grateful for my assistance.

"This is where we last saw him," he explained as he pointed toward a cul-de-sac. "That was about an hour ago. He ran east in this cul-de-sac toward the woods over there."

"Where is the house that was burglarized?" I asked. I needed to collect scent material from the burglary scene in order to search for the suspect.

"It's about a mile and a half south of here," the sergeant replied, "but we think we have him boxed in right here somewhere. We just need you to start from here and see if you can find him in these woods."

I knew that what I was about to say was not going to be appreciated. These officers had been on the scene, guarding their perimeter, for over an hour. They were no doubt expecting me to conduct a rapid search for the suspect so they could get it over with. Although it is often part of the job, most cops don't do well standing around and waiting for hours. Theirs can be the most exciting, adrenaline-filled job in the world, and it makes the sit-and-wait periods that much harder. What's more, I was a female campus cop with a goofy-looking hound. I doubted they'd appreciate me telling this seasoned sergeant how to run his investigation.

Unfortunately, I was going to have to do it anyway.

"I need to start my dog at the crime scene," I said apologetically.

"But that's a mile and a half down the road," the sergeant protested. "Can't you just send him in here? We know he went down this street."

I had to give the sergeant a quick lesson in the difference between patrol dog "tracking" and bloodhound "trailing." First of all, I explained, A.J. was trained to find a *specific* person, but he needed the scent of that person to do it. Even more important, I told the sergeant, bloodhound trailing was considered evidence admissible in court. If A.J. trailed the suspect's scent from the crime scene, it would be incriminating evidence that could help convict the burglar. If we started from elsewhere, the value of his testimony would be lost.

I knew the sergeant would not want to keep the officers at their posts for much longer. This would mean paying more overtime as well as delaying other calls for service. I waited for his response, hoping he would understand my reasoning.

Finally, he agreed to let me handle the search my way. "Follow Officer Hohmann here. He'll take you to the crime scene. He can run as your backup, too."

I thanked him and followed behind Officer Hohmann's patrol car for over a mile to the crime scene. The beautiful, mansion-like homes were located in a new subdivision. The price tag on the homes in this area started at over eight hundred thousand dollars. I pulled in behind Officer Hohmann's patrol car in front of the model home.

Officer Hohmann walked up to meet me.

"Hi there," he said, extending his hand. "I'm John."

"Thanks for backing me up," I said as I shook his hand. "Let me grab A.J. so we can get to work." John followed me to the back of my truck.

"Cool-looking dog," John said. "I hope he can find this guy."

I explained that though A.J. had found people before, we couldn't make any promises.

"What do you need me to do?"

"I need for you to be my eyes," I explained. "I will be busy watching A.J. all the time. I need to rely on you to cover me and to watch my back. Stay close to me, to warn me if you see something I need to know about. And understand that I won't be a part of the arrest team. If we find this guy, I'll back out with the dog and let you go in to make the arrest."

"Sounds good," John said.

"I'll need to collect scent from the point of entry," I said. "I'll use a sterile gauze pad but will be careful not to wipe away any fingerprints. Can you show me where he got into the house?"

John led me to the back of the house where the suspect had crawled through a bathroom window. I canvassed the interior of the house to look for any other possible sources of scent. Although the model home had been unoccupied, it contained gorgeous furniture. The burglar had tracked mud into the house, leaving muddy footprints all over the white carpet. Items had been broken and scattered all over the floor. Beer cans were strewn throughout the house. The side and back windows of the home had been shot out with a pellet or BB gun. Eight other homes within the cul-de-sac had also had windows shot out. At the time, it could not be confirmed that the vandalism of the other houses was tied to this particular burglary. Any fingerprint evidence at the crime scene would take weeks, perhaps months, to process in order to identify a suspect. All hopes for an immediate capture in this case rested squarely on A.J.'s ability to find the suspect who was likely hiding in the woods over a mile away.

I set a sterile gauze pad on top of the windowsill where the suspect had entered, allowing about five minutes for it to absorb the scent particles. While we waited, John told me the details of the incident. "A citizen called to report a suspicious person after seeing a guy carrying a television set down the street. That was at four this morning," John explained. "The first officer on the scene saw the suspect carrying the television and confronted him. The suspect dropped the TV and ran up into the woods. We searched for him but couldn't find him. We checked around the area and discovered the burglary. Then, at six this morning, one of the officers spotted the suspect again."

"Was that second sighting where I just met with the sergeant?" I asked.

"Yes," John said. "He took off running east into that cul-de-sac toward the woods after he spotted the patrol car. Because he hid earlier, we think he's probably still hiding now."

While we talked, A.J. kept looking up at me in anticipation. His tongue lolled out the side of his mouth and his tail wagged slowly. He knew he was getting ready to search because I was in uniform and he was in his harness. He just couldn't understand why I was taking so long. I reached down and scratched him under his collar. I removed the gauze pad from the windowsill and was ready to start A.J. "Don't tell me where the TV was found," I instructed John. I wanted to see if I could figure it out by just watching A.J.'s body language. There would be a scent pool, a large area filled with a concentration of invisible adrenaline scent where the suspect had initially been caught off guard, right where he realized that he was caught and dropped the television. I snapped a long line into A.J.'s harness and prepared to start him on the search. "You ready?" I asked John, who was standing behind me.

"You bet," John responded.

The scent-laden gauze pad was resting on top of a plastic bag to prevent it from coming into contact with any ground scent. A.J. was eagerly straining to reach the gauze pad. I held him by his nylon collar and eased forward toward the white square. It never ceased to amaze me that such a tiny piece of material—a three-by-five piece of cotton mesh—could provide information that could actually save a life or put someone in prison. I felt the butterflies flutter in my stomach as I pointed at the gauze pad and released my hold on A.J.'s collar. A.J. moved forward and eagerly sniffed the gauze pad.

"Search!" I commanded. A.J. picked up a scent trail leading out of the unfenced backyard. As I watched his body language, I could tell that he was on it. In cases where he could not find the scent, he would let me know by making eye contact with me and shaking himself off. But he was moving forward and pulling in the harness and we were on our way. He made a sharp left turn through the muddy side yard of a neighboring home. I pulled A.J. to a halt for a moment.

"Look at this," I said to John as I pointed to the distinct shoe tracks in the mud. The prints were heading toward as well as away from the house that had been burglarized. They appeared to be a match to the tennis shoe mud transfer that was left on the floor in the kitchen of the burglarized home. A.J. was, in fact, on the trail of our suspect. The track evidence served to boost my confidence and the butterfly activity.

"Goooood boooooy," I encouraged A.J., as I allowed him to continue to work the scent. A.J. trailed out into the cul-de-sac where the other homes had been vandalized. They were all unoccupied and under construction. After sniffing around the vandalized homes, A.J. worked north and wanted to crawl under a barbed-wire fence that led into a vacant field. The weeds on both sides of the fence were flattened, an indication that someone had crawled through already. Under most circumstances, we would have limboed our way under the fence and found a way to lift A.J. over. This was risking injury, both to ourselves and my dog. I noticed a break in the fence facing the street that would allow us to walk around the barbed-wire to the other side. Once past the fence, A.J. picked up the scent again and worked toward the section of road where the suspect had dropped the television. He was heading toward the cud-de-sac where the suspect was last seen.

A.J. worked at his ambling pace as John and I jogged along behind him. Suddenly, my hound stopped, lifted his nose high, began wagging his tail like a windshield wiper, and turned around. With his tail still wagging, A.J. started working away from the road and up an embankment into thick brush. There was a noticeable change in his body language.

"Was this where the television was dropped?" I asked.

"Yes it was!" John said in amazement. "Look at him. He really can tell, can't he?"

"Right now he's within a cloud of scent called a scent pool," I explained. "This usually means the suspect stayed in that location for some time and that there's a large amount of scent in the area."

I allowed A.J. to work through the scent pool. I had been told that the suspect dropped the television and disappeared into the brush just east of the roadway. Immediately to the east the ground rose in a steep embankment. After checking the flat area, A.J. started to climb east up the muddy embankment, dragging me up the hill behind him. The vegetation and the dirt had been disturbed there, confirming that A.J. was working directly on the trail the suspect had taken.

"I've got the suspect's tracks up here!" I yelled. "Do you want to follow us?"

No sooner were the words out of my mouth than I saw the backpack. A.J. had stopped on the trail and was hovering over an object. His tail was wagging madly as he sniffed and happily slobbered all over a green backpack that had been discarded in the middle of the steep trail.

"I've got a backpack. What do you want me to do with it?" Normally, before physical evidence can be moved from a crime scene, it is photographed. But because the perpetrator was still in the area, we were working under exigent circumstances. The contents of the backpack might provide information critical to the investigation.

"Hand it to me," John said. I picked up the backpack and swung it down to John. He had already radioed in that A.J. had found the suspect's tracks. Now two plainclothes detectives drove up to our location and joined John.

"Wow!" one of the detectives exclaimed as John handed him the backpack. "This dog is hot!"

"Good boooooy," I praised A.J. as the detectives opened the backpack. It was like opening a treasure chest. The contents included CO^2 cartridges for a BB gun; two cans of Keystone beer, the same brand found inside the burglarized home; a blue automobile dashboard cover; and a wallet. The wallet contained no less than the driver's license of our suspect. A.J. had not only located critical evidence; he had given our suspect a name and a face. I was ecstatic. Now all we had to do was find where he was hiding.

"Should I continue to work up this embankment?" I asked John. The terrain was very steep and unsafe. There was no telling just how far the suspect had gone in that direction.

"Let's take A.J. up the street," John said, pointing north. "There were four cars broken into in a business-complex parking lot between here and where the suspect is hiding in the woods. One of the cars is blue. This blue dashboard cover could have been taken from that car. Can we see if your dog alerts on the car?"

"You bet," I agreed. I pulled A.J. from the muddy trail and guided him back down to the roadway.

"Go catch this guy," one of the detectives said as he gave A.J. a friendly pat on the rump. I beamed with pride. A.J. was doing an outstanding job.

Walking him by his collar so that he understood he was not trailing, John and I took A.J. a short distance up the road. We stopped just south of the entrance to the parking lot. This was only about a hundred yards north of where A.J. had found the backpack. I released my hold on A.J.'s collar and gave a slight tug on the harness. This was his cue that I was about to expect him to get back to work again. Thanks to his training, A.J. was accustomed to stopping on the trail and then picking right up where he had left off in another location.

"Get to work," I commanded A.J. as he pulled hard into his harness. He immediately began to work the scent north along the roadside. As he approached the business-complex driveway, A.J. made a right turn and cut east down into the parking lot. He worked around the cars that had been burglarized but did not show interest in any specific car. Since he didn't alert on any of the burglarized cars in the lot, there was no way to connect the blue dashboard cover to the car burglaries. A.J. worked back to the front of the building and began trotting along the sidewalk as he continued north. We were heading back toward the area where the sergeant and other officers last saw the suspect.

We approached the intersection where the sergeant was still waiting with the other officers. The suspect had been seen running east into the cul-de-sac toward the woods. A.J. ignored the sergeant and the police officers and made a right turn, heading east. Another uniformed officer joined John as my backup and jogged along behind us as A.J. continued to work the scent.

To my surprise, A.J. suddenly turned and worked north into the yard of a house located right at the corner of the cul-de-sac. He showed intense interest in the front and side yard of the house. Then he started working away from the yard down into an area of dense brush and prickling, snaky berry vines.

"Was the suspect last seen running into the woods over there?" I asked in confusion. The yard we were in was right next to the road and within earshot of where the sergeant and other officers had been standing for the last few hours. It didn't seem possible that the suspect could have been right there, listening to the officer's conversations.

"No," the sergeant yelled over to me. "We didn't actually see him run into the woods. He was last seen running east from the main road. He could be anywhere in this cul-de-sac or in the woods."

A.J. continued to pull me down into the berry vines and heavy brush. Both my backup officers stopped, reluctant to follow A.J. on this very rough terrain, but I continued to follow and trust my dog. Suddenly, A.J. stopped and began his customary end-of-the-trail "butt wag." This violent wagging of his rear end was reserved for the happy occasion when he had located his quarry, when he knew he was about to receive a hearty chest rub. I peered through the brush and saw that A.J. was sniffing the denim pant leg of a man curled up behind a log!

My backup officers were waiting fifteen yards behind me. They had not wanted to follow me into the maze of prickly vines and poison oak. They were fearless when it came to confronting a potentially violent felony suspect—but hesitant to be exposed to an itchy rash. I jerked A.J. backward with my left hand and drew my 9mm Glock pistol with my right.

"Freeze!" I screamed as loud as I could, throwing in "If you move, my dog will bite you!" for good measure. There was absolutely nothing threatening in A.J.'s demeanor, but I hoped this guy would take my word for it. The suspect did not budge. John and the other officer, having heard my shout, came crashing through the brush as I kept the suspect in the front site of my pistol. They moved in front of me and engaged the suspect as I holstered my gun and pulled A.J. back. Three other officers rushed past me and crashed down into the brush as I climbed out with A.J.

"Great job!" a plainclothes detective said as I walked out of the brush with A.J. My adrenaline and excitement were at an all-time high.

"Thank you," I managed as I tried to catch my breath. One of the uniformed officers stooped over and started to pet A.J. "You have a great dog there," the detective said.

"I'd like to see if A.J. will make an identification on the suspect if I could," I said.

"What do you mean?" asked the detective.

"When he finds the person he has been tracking, A.J. will go up to that specific person, sit and place his paw on his or her thigh. This is the form of identification he is trained to do. It is known as a 'scent lineup' and is admissible in court."

I knew that the detectives and officers in Scotts Valley had never seen or heard of a scent lineup. But I wanted to give A.J. the chance to finish his trail and to identify the person whose scent he had been tracking if, in fact, it was actually him.

"Are you serious?" the detective asked. "How come I've never heard of this?"

"Probably because this method and bloodhounds are used mainly on the East Coast," I said. "It takes a few years to perfect a dog in this method of scent discrimination. Most police dog trainers primarily train dogs in tracking, not in scent discrimination trailing. Can we give it a try and see what A.J. does?"

"You bet," said the detective. "This I have to see."

During the arrest, the suspect had fought with John and the other officers and had been subdued with pepper spray. Now John, his uniform a bit disheveled and covered with dirt and weeds, was leading the handcuffed suspect up to the driveway of the nearest house. The suspect's eyes were swollen shut, his face beet red from the burning effects of the pepper spray. His clothing was wet from water that had been used to flush the irritant from his eyes.

"I need several people to stand around him on either side," I instructed. "Stand still and don't talk to the dog while he's working." The officers formed a semicircle in the driveway with the suspect standing near the middle. There were a total of eleven people standing in the scent lineup.

"What's going on?" I heard the suspect ask in confusion. He couldn't see what was happening.

"Shut up and stand still!" one of the officers growled.

I led A.J. to the end of the driveway, snapped his lead into his harness, and commanded him to "get to work." He eagerly trotted up the driveway toward the group of "suspects" and went into an immediate butt-wag, indicating that he was in the scent pool of the person he had been trailing. A.J. ignored the uniformed officers and the plainclothes detectives and focused his attention on the suspect. He tried to make eye contact with his quarry, but the suspect's eyes were still swollen shut. Because pepper spray is a contact irritant and not an aerosol that forms a potent cloud (like mace), it had no effect on A.J. He happily sat down in front of our suspect and placed his paw on the man's leg. There was a loud round of applause from the crowd of cops.

I beamed with pride as I praised my dog, "Good boooooy!" I knelt in front of A.J. and scratched his floppy ears, and then gave him a much-deserved chest rub. A few of the officers walked by and thanked me, smiling at A.J., who was moaning with pleasure, oblivious to anyone else. It was one of the happiest moments of my life. A.J. had fulfilled my dream of hunting down a felony suspect. My dog, a dog who couldn't even walk on a leash and who was terrified to touch carpet when I brought him home, had surefootedly tracked this man and found both critical physical evidence *and* the perpetrator of the crime. The entire case was solved based on our work. The suspect, who had the same name as the driver's license inside the backpack, eventually "rolled over" and confessed to the burglary.

A.J. and I made our way back to my truck, with the thanks and congratulations of the officers on the scene still ringing in my ears. "I'm so proud of you," I said as I bent down to scratch his chin and chest. "You are *such* a good dog!" A.J. stood, stoic as usual, then nuzzled just a little bit against me, vying for another ear rub.

"Up you go," I commanded, grasping his collar in my right hand and using my left hand to tap his left leg. As all my dogs were trained to do, A.J. lifted his left leg, set it down on my left hand which was hovering about a foot above the ground, and I hoisted him up onto the tailgate of my truck. He climbed into his crate, ready for the ride home. "Are you looking for this?" I asked, and forked over the much-deserved cheddar cheese treat.

I grinned to myself all the way home.

It had been a perfect search.

Chapter Six
PET HUNTER

Not long after our big case in Scotts Valley, A.J. decided to wander off again. It was a day that ultimately changed my life. My sister Debbie and niece Jenny came to visit me in my cabin, and instead of keeping A.J. inside and worrying that he'd slobber all over my guests (a social failing most bloodhounds share), I walked him and Rachel outside and put them both in the dog run just outside my front door. I seldom put my dogs inside this makeshift holding cell (they led spoiled indoor lives) but the run was set in a cool, shady area within a grove of tall redwoods, and not a bad place at all for a dog nap. Inside, we had lunch and laughed as we watched a rented movie.

Then Rachel started barking. I was irritated—it was just like her to decide she wanted to be invited to the party, too. I knew she was just trying to get my attention, so I tried to tune her out.

But when the barking got louder and more insistent, I knew better than to ignore it.

When I approached the kennel, I couldn't believe my eyes. At the base of the kennel was a large hole, big enough for a bloodhound to squeeze through—on the inside was a large mound of dirt. A.J. had dug a hole under the fence and crawled out. When I saw that he was gone, I felt guilt, sorrow, fear, panic—a rush of emotions too overwhelming to be sorted out. There were miles and miles of forest around the cabin, but the woods were crisscrossed with roads, and I was certain that if A.J. encountered a highway, and if he was busy sniffing whatever scent had inspired him to dig out of his kennel, he was darned sure not going to stop and look both ways.

I knew I wasn't going to be able to track down my dog by myself. Because of my years of police training, I knew I needed to put my feelings aside and get down to business. So I did what I had done five years earlier, what any good bloodhound-handling police officer would do: bring in a search dog. I threw open the gate of the kennel and let Rachel out. "Go find A.J.!" I shouted. It had worked five years earlier when Rachel rescued A.J. from the scary thunder—maybe it would work again.

Rachel took off, made a loop around the yard, and returned with a stick in her mouth. She looked at me, and it was clear that she wanted to play and didn't know what I wanted. She wasn't going to be able to help me. Rachel had not been on a search in a long time, and it would have been very unfair to ask her to summon up her unused skills in that moment and find her friend. Someone else would have to do it.

Feeling every tick of the clock, I imagined how far A.J. could have gotten already and how many different directions he might have taken. I called Greg Almos, the team leader with the Santa Cruz Sheriff's search-and-rescue team.

"A.J. is lost!" I blurted out when Greg answered his phone. "I need volunteers to come help me find him." Surely, after all of the hours I'd invested in training with that team and all of the searches A.J. had worked for them, there would be an immediate response to help us.

"I'm so sorry," Greg said. "We're only authorized to launch a search for people. We can't search for lost pets."

I was dismayed, but I understood the limitations of departmental policies. If Greg and the other search-and-rescue team volunteers had been authorized, they would've come and helped me find A.J.

Then I had another idea. I called my friend, Jeanne Mason, who I'd helped to train her working search dog. Jeanne was not home, but her daughter, Stacey Dorsey, was. Within an hour, Stacey was beside me, with her mother's golden retriever Kea in harness, ready to track A.J.'s scent.

We used the blanket inside A.J.'s wire kennel as our scent article. I pulled the dirty blue blanket out of the dog crate and set it on the ground directly in front of the spot where A.J. had dug out. Kea was a seasoned search-and-rescue, or SAR, dog with a successful record of finding lost people. She and A.J. had worked together on many middle-of-the-night searches throughout the Santa Cruz Mountains. I already knew how clear a scent trail could be to a working search dog. What I did not know was whether Kea would be able to follow a dog's scent, too.

A.J. was a treasured member of my family. He was my police partner, my pride and joy, my tear-stained cheek wiper, and my dear friend. If he was lost forever, I could not fathom how I would manage life without him.

It was hard to believe that after all the searches I had conducted with A.J. wrapped in his harness and tethered to me by a lead, suddenly *he* was the one that needed to be tracked. I doubted that he was capable of getting lost—his sense of smell was far too fine-tuned for that, but I knew he might walk in front of a car, or that someone might take him in and decide to keep him.

As I raced along behind Stacey and Kea, trying to keep my panic in check, I couldn't help but think of the times when, as a police dispatcher, I had turned down desperate pet owners who had called for assistance. They'd called 9-1-1 when their pets were missing, and I had followed protocol and politely told them 9-1-1 was not designed to help pets—just people. That cartoon image of a fire crew coming in their ladder truck to rescue a kitten from a tree just does not happen; neither time nor budget constraints will allow it.

As a police K-9 handler, I'd taken even more calls from frantic pet owners who had hoped I could use my bloodhound to help find a lost cat or dog. I remembered one of those calls vividly: A woman involved in a rollover car crash on a busy, mountainous highway had lost her Siamese cat in the dense forest. Her plastic cat carrier had broken open and the cat took off into the unfamiliar woods in a panic. The woman pleaded with me to bring A.J. out to track her lost cat. But because considerable time is spent teaching search dogs to *ignore* the scent of cats and other dogs, the answer was (and still is today for other law enforcement search dogs) the same: *Sorry, but no.*

I was sympathetic, and explained why I could not help her, but after I hung up the phone, I joked with one of my coworkers that someone actually had the audacity to ask me to use A.J. to track a cat! Because A.J. had a successful track record in finding people, it seemed crazy to consider it. Little did I know at the time how prophetic my statement would be!

But suddenly, I understood. Now that it was *my* dog missing, I felt deep empathy for that woman. Had she ever found her cat? How many people could access the resource I had—a trained search dog, in harness and ready to work, within an hour of the lost pet's disappearance? Most would be reduced to circling the neighborhood, helplessly calling their lost pet's name, fingers crossed, knowing the odds were against them.

That, I told myself, would *not* be the case with A.J. I had to find him. He was not just a pet. He was a valuable law enforcement tool; a well-trained working dog. But more importantly to me, he was the puppy project I had taken on, even though his future as a working dog had seemed doomed from day one. In our five years together, he had become a full-fledged member of my little family. He snored at my feet at night. He serenaded me with a bellowing melody of *rooooo, rooooo* every morning as I fixed his breakfast. And the only thing A.J. ever asked of me was nothing more than an ear massage or chest rub.

I could not lose him now.

Stacey and I jogged behind Kea as she followed the scent trail west along the road directly in front of my cabin. Instead of traveling deep into the woods in a meandering, zigzag pattern as I expected he would do, A.J. had stayed on the roadway.

Kea trotted along but suddenly stopped, turned herself around, and then made a hard right and headed north on a private roadway. As Kea jogged down the road to where it intersected another private, dirt road at the bottom of the hill, Stacey and I hurried behind her.

By the time she reached the intersection, Kea was at a run, straining at the leash. I stopped for a second to catch my breath.

And there, on the porch of a cabin up ahead, happily sniffing at a stack of boxes, was my wonderful, rotten, naughty, missing dog.

"A.J.!" I called, tears of relief running down my face as I approached him. He jerked his head around and began wagging his tail at our little search party. He often worked and trained with Kea, and he was delighted to see her. He stood still while I snapped a leash to his collar and checked him for injuries. He was soaking wet, evidence that he had gone farther north than this road and had taken a swim in the creek, but he was unharmed.

"What were you *thinking?*" I demanded. "Why would you do such a thing?"

But there was no point in chastising him. There was no way A.J. could know what he had just put me through. He was happy to come home with us, and I thanked God we had found him.

I turned to Stacey. "I can't thank you enough. I owe you."

Stacey smiled. "I know you would've done it for us if Kea was missing."

We walked in silence back toward my cabin.

"Who'd have believed we'd have to bring in a golden retriever to rescue the missing bloodhound?" I joked as we made our way up my driveway. I went inside and handed A.J.'s leash to my sister who was shocked to see us so soon. Debbie admonished A.J. and stroked his pendulous ears while I groped through the refrigerator for a suitable treat for Kea. A hunk of cheddar cheese did not seem a sufficient reward to me, but Kea was pretty happy about it. Stacey, who was late for an appointment, packed up the hero dog that had found my precious hound and left, my chatter of gratitude and praise following her to the road.

Soon after, Debbie and Jenny packed up their things and headed back to Fresno. As I watched them leave, I was exhausted. The panic and fear had literally drained all my energy. Alone in the cabin, I poured myself a cup of coffee, settled into a chair on my deck, and took a few minutes to digest what had just happened.

At this point in my career, I had been involved in scent training dogs for more than eight years. During that time, I had never once heard of dogs being used to search for missing pets. I knew of dogs that were used to find bombs, drugs, food, termites, natural gas, minerals, turtle eggs, even cancer cells. Judging from my experience, and by what I'd observed in other working dogs, it seemed that there was no end to a dog's search capabilities—*any* scent that could be recognized, a well-trained dog could learn to find.

So why hadn't anyone tried using a trained search dog to find lost pets? I knew I wasn't the only dog handler who had received requests to track lost cats that had run off into the woods. Searching for lost pets would be a natural extension of the other jobs that search dogs undertook. Long before they were ever used to find people buried in an avalanche, submerged under water, or trapped under a collapsed building, bloodhounds and other canines had been used to track animal scent, centuries before they were trained to locate people. Most of all, searching for lost pets was certainly a service for which there was a need. For millions of people, a pet—whether dog, cat, parrot, iguana, or pot-bellied pig—is much more than just an animal that shares a living space. Sometime after the moment of adoption—or the morning when the pet shows up unannounced with "keep me" written all over its face and wagging tail—it becomes a family member.

In my house, with A.J., it had happened years ago, when I'd realized that his fears and health problems and total unpreparedness to become a working dog no longer mattered. Long before he started showing promise as a search dog, A.J. won my heart just by showing me that nothing in this world made him happier than sitting beside me, schmoozing for a scratch, moaning when I rubbed his chest or massaged his itchy ears. He wasn't the slump against you sort of dog, he wasn't giddy or affectionate, and his kind of cute was the type only a mother can love. But A.J. loved me, and he trusted me, and so somewhere along the way all his "flaws" started looking like charming quirks of character. I loved him more than I could even explain.

Unfortunately, when a pet goes missing, the perception that it's a bona fide family member doesn't hold up. When a child disappears, the community throws all its resources into bringing him or her safely home. When a beloved dog or cat disappears, it's just that: LOST DOG, two words on a poster that most people won't even notice.

Somebody ought to train a search dog to find lost pets, I thought.

Guess which somebody it turned out to be . . .

Chapter Seven
THE ROAD LESS TRAVELED

I would probably never have become a pet detective if it hadn't been for Rachel, my once successful search dog turned eighty-pound couch slouch. If I hadn't retired her, I wouldn't have had a nagging sense that she was subliminally shouting, "Pick me! Pick me!" every time the idea of training a dog to search for lost pets crossed my mind.

At first, I had hoped someone else would do it. I'd logged on to an Internet chat group of search dog trainers and thrown my idea out with confidence that it was genius: "Why doesn't someone train a dog to search for lost pets?" I waited for the flood of "What a great idea"-type replies to appear in my mailbox. But instead, e-mails of negativity, not creativity, began to flow my way. At first, the normally chatty group was dead silent. Then someone wrote: "Why would anyone want to ruin a good search dog by training it to search for lost pets?" Another trainer jumped in, "We all know how long it takes to train a search dog—why would we waste time training one to find lost pets?"

I had thought that by putting the idea out into the search-and-rescue world, I'd be rid of it. But it was obvious after the silence, which spoke volumes, and then those two e-mails that *that* was not going to happen.

It was then that I learned that the bulk of the search-and-rescue community considered tracking lost pets to be taboo. It wasn't that my peers considered the idea to be impossible—most just considered it to be beneath them. There was a guiding principle that training a search-and-rescue dog to search for lost pets would ruin the dog because it could never be used to search for humans again. That's because a search dog could easily be confused if expected to search for a cat one day and ignore the passing child and then search for the child the next day and ignore the neighbor's cat. It would be especially difficult if the only scent article available for a lost child was a pillowcase touched by the family cat. Since human lives depended on it, search-and-rescue dogs should never be used to search for lost pets. I agreed with this principle. I was fully prepared that if I did train one of my search dogs to find lost pets, I would never use that dog for law enforcement purposes again. What I wasn't prepared for was how most of the other search dog handlers reacted—as if I was out of my mind.

But how I would be received by my peers didn't change the fact that I knew *someone* should give this a try. I didn't think it would be ruining a good dog at all. It would be giving a dog a great job. And it would be the beginning of availability of a valuable service—one that is already in place around the world to locate lost people but nonexistent for pets. Of course, *I* had a full time job as a police officer and two bloodhounds to work and train—and not a minute to spend on a "pet project" that would involve the kind of time and energy training a four-legged pet detective would take. I was way too busy to do it myself. And I wouldn't have, if it hadn't been for Rachel.

I hadn't worked her in more than two years. When my focus had shifted from searching for evidence to trailing criminals with bloodhounds, I had retired her. I hated to do it, but there was no way I could train three dogs in two different specialties (or so I thought). It made sense to keep Rachel, who was the oldest and the only non-bloodhound of the group, at home.

Even though she had less of my time, Rachel continued to share my life in a way the bloodhounds never could. They were my companions and my coworkers and I loved them to death, but Rachel was special. As my first search-and-rescue dog, she would always have a special piece of my heart. A.J. and Chase were both afflicted with the bloodhound curse of nonstop drool. Because they were so messy, they were usually confined behind wooden baby gates—albeit in their own bedroom, so they didn't have it *too* bad.

Rachel had one of those wiggle-butt dog personalities that won over even people who didn't like dogs. She was quiet when she should be, she knew when to lie down and get out of the way, and she loved nothing more than to sit and let anyone pet her. And because of her sweet nature, I had no shortage of friends who volunteered to keep Rachel when I took the bloodhounds out of town on training exercises—I had a list of people who would gladly take her for the weekend, or forever, if I wasn't careful to pick her up before she wormed her way too far into their lives.

At night, the bloodhounds slept inside their individual kennels with blankets to cover the wire-grate doors. The kennels were their dens and they looked forward to going inside— probably because they finagled a treat out of me every night when I put them in. Rachel had no such bedtime routine. I did have a crate that I could have put her in, but for the most part, she slept on my bed, curled up next to my shoulder. She occupied the place where a second pillow—and the head of a husband (if I had ever found one)—would have rested.

The only flaw in this sleeping arrangement was Rachel's great affection for breakfast – and the timetable on which she felt it should be served. Sunrise, whether at 7 A.M. or 5:30, meant breakfast to her. Every day, the moment the first gleam of sunlight hit the window, Rachel would leap off the bed, ready to eat.

She never licked me. She never pushed me with her paw or annoyed me with hot, smelly dog breath. And I never woke up to find a dog staring at me. Instead, Rachel woke me up with a unique whining noise. It was actually more of a moan than a whine—a sound Rachel used when she wanted something and a signature method of begging that had long since earned her the nickname "Mona."

I would awake to an obnoxious "mmmmmmmmm, mmmmmmmm" noise, and the battle of wills would begin. Rachel wanted food; I wanted more sleep. I would use my best, most forceful whisper—the kind mothers use to hush their children in public—to tell her to "go lay DOWN," but it only served to wake up the bloodhounds. And A.J., as if in cahoots with Rachel to get me up, would start in with his own set of obnoxious noises. While Chase patiently waited in silence, A.J. would rake his dog nails on the wire grate of his crate, creating a metallic "chinggggg." When I had finally had enough of the chinging and moaning, I would give in, get up, and begin my day, Rachel having demonstrated, again, that her life revolved around food. I knew she would do anything, and search for anything, for a bite to eat.

Which brought me, morning after morning, to the thought that *my* underused, over-motivated dog was the best dog to take a shot at learning to search for pets, and to the logical conclusion that the *somebody* who ought to train a dog to do this was none other than me.

As weeks passed, I started to mentally move past the "who" part of this idea, since it was increasingly obvious that it would be Rachel and me, and began to dwell on the "how" angle. Rachel had always loved search work, but I knew this training process would be different. No training manual existed (at that time) to tell me how to teach my dog to trail the scent of another dog. There wasn't an instructor or mentor I could call for pointers on search strategy when searching for a lost cat. There wasn't a Web site, training videos, or even the ability to ask questions on an Internet e-mail list (where my idea had already been rejected). Rachel and I would be alone in this endeavor.

Even though I wasn't sure it could be done, I knew that if any dog could be trained to locate lost pets, it was Rachel. She wasn't just on my mind because she was unemployed and begging for breakfast every morning. She was, as strange as it may sound, an animal lover in her own right. As a search dog, it had been her one clear flaw. Her mad passion for tracking, trailing, and sniffing all of God's furry, four-legged creatures—even during a training exercise or when I was desperately trying to demonstrate to a bunch of jaded cops that my dog and I knew our stuff—was an embarrassment to me more than once.

We'd be working along, focused and professional as could be, and then Rachel would spy or smell a cat, a rabbit, or, worst of all a skunk, and she'd morph in a heartbeat from a disciplined, super sniffing search dog to a big dopey critter-hunting mutt. One instructor had even gone so far as to tell me I needed to put a shock collar on Rachel to break her of her "critter problem," but I didn't have the heart. Instead, I resorted to yelling, *"LEAVE IT!"* at her and she happily ignored me as she loped around on her bunny hunt.

Rachel never actually chased critters – she simply hunted for their scent so that she could freeze and point them out to me. When she picked up a forbidden animal scent, Rachel's tail would immediately wiggle in uncontrollable excitement. Her body would crouch low to the ground as she developed a sudden intensity about her work. She would cast back and forth until she zeroed in on the source of the scent. Once she had found the animal, Rachel would freeze in place. Sometimes she lifted a paw in a classic pointer stance, but most times she just stood on all fours, motionless like a statue as she stared at the concealed critter. If the bunny or cat bolted and ran, Rachel would not take chase but instead she would stay behind, wiggling as she inhaled the intoxicating odors.

Since Rachel's passion for other animals had always been a professional burden for both of us, I couldn't help thinking that if she were actually searching for pets, her longstanding Achilles' heel would probably work to both of our advantage.

As if she knew she was being considered for her dream job, Rachel seemed to make a point of reminding me how her talents were withering away. Several times a day, during the months that I pondered my pet detective idea, she'd post herself at the glass doors in my kitchen, facing the woods behind the cabin. She'd stare intently at squirrels that would descend down the massive trunks of the two redwood trees my deck was built into. The squirrels came, along with a flock of obnoxious blue jays, to gather at the wooden bird feeder that I kept stocked, primarily for the sake of entertaining my dog.

Watching the bird feeder activity was addictive for Rachel. I loved to see her come to life when she saw the animals there. I'd say, "bird-bird" when there was a bird or a squirrel at the feeder, and Rachel would leap off the couch like a gazelle but then creep slyly, like a panther, up to the glass door. She would freeze in a bird-dog stance, lick her lips in anticipation, and eventually roll her eyes over to me, showing me what a smart, capable, pointer she could be. *"Isn't this GREAT?"* she seemed to be asking.

One day in the late fall of 1996, I finally took the hint. I had put off my idea for long enough. "Do you want to work?" I asked Rachel. This question was actually a motivational command that I had used for Rachel's search work. It was designed to pump her with adrenaline just prior to letting go of her collar and sending her out to search. Her flying leap off the couch and wiggling tail were a decisive *"YES!"* It was my day off and I had nothing planned. I was ready to get started.

The only problem was, I wasn't sure *where* to start. I knew that Rachel would always know what the command "Search!" meant. And I knew that she would attempt to find whatever scent I presented under her nose. What I didn't know was how capable she would be of recognizing a specific animal's scent. Did one cat smell like all *other* cats? Or did each cat have its own unique scent just as humans do? I decided to begin by letting Rachel search for my cat, Yogi. If she could pull that off, we'd move on to something more sophisticated.

Poor Yogi. She was a good-natured cat, but definitely not playful. I'm sure she would never have volunteered to be bait for Rachel. But whatever lack of enthusiasm Yogi had for Rachel was certainly not mutual. Rachel loved Yogi. She loved to watch "her" kitty go about her life in and outside the cabin.

Rachel rarely bothered Yogi, but she was always admiring her from afar. Yogi was a faded orange, cream-color tabby with a distant personality. She didn't like people, dogs, or anything that moved—except mice. She didn't like to be petted or held. She seemed to like me when I fed her, but she didn't really involve herself deeply in my life.

My plan was to put Yogi in her breadbox-size cat crate, hide her in the woods, and see if Rachel could find her. But Yogi didn't want to go into her crate. Unlike the dogs, who associated their crates with yummy snacks and peaceful slumber, Yogi associated her purple plastic prison with a trip to the dreaded veterinarian.

Leaving Rachel inside the cabin, I found Yogi lounging outside in a patch of ivy, picked her up, and pushed her unhappy feline fanny into her crate with a soft blanket inside for her to snuggle with. It was a gorgeous sunny day in the redwoods—I figured that even in the worst case scenario, Rachel (if not Yogi) and I would spend some time enjoying the outdoors.

Before I hid the crate, I carried it with me as I walked all around the wooded area surrounding my cabin. This allowed me to disperse my scent, and Yogi's scent, throughout the entire area. If I had simply walked out, set the crate in a hiding place and walked back to Rachel, she would have cheated and followed *my* scent back to the point where I had planted my cat. Search dogs are smart and use their brains in addition to their noses. I tucked Yogi's crate in a stand of trees about one hundred yards from the cabin and camouflaged it with a towel and some leaves. Then I turned my attention to Rachel.

Her black nylon harness was buried at the bottom of a box of search supplies that hadn't been touched for more than two years. I had to adjust the straps a bit to fit Rachel's retirement-widened girth, but she couldn't have cared less. She was getting more hyped up by the minute at the thought of working again.

As I always did when I worked her, I told Rachel to sit and then snapped my thirty-foot-long lead to the D-ring on her harness. I held her collar with my left hand, brought my right hand up under her nose with a bit of Yogi's fur between my fingers, and I commanded her, "Take scent."

I will never forget Rachel's reaction. Normally, she'd sniff the scent item, then strain forward, ready to work. But on that afternoon in the forest, she sniffed the cat fur and made a face as close to a smile as a Weimaraner can manage, then swung her whole head around to look me right in the eyes – questioning, I'm sure, if I had made some sort of mistake or if she'd hit the search dog's equivalent of a jackpot. *Find a cat and earn cheese?* It was a doggy dream come true!

"Where's the kitty?" I asked her. Rachel knew what the word "kitty" meant. She snapped her attention back in front of her, ears pricked forward and weight shifting from one front foot to the other. She was ready to go.

"Are you ready?" I said, grinning at her excitement. This caused Rachel to glance back around and make eye contact with me one more time. If a dog could talk, Rachel would have been shouting at me, saying, "YES! *F-i-n-a-l-l-y*!" I'm sure she wondered why, stupid human that I was, I had wasted so much time asking her to find guns and body parts and why it had taken me this long to figure out that she'd rather find cats and rabbits.

"Search!" I commanded. Rachel lunged forward and hit the end of the harness, pulling me behind her. Even though I had presented Rachel with Yogi's scent using a tuft of her fur, I was not going to work this as a scent-discrimination trailing assignment. We were not going to try to follow Yogi's scent trail; instead, I was going to work Rachel in a scent detection, or "area search," mode. This meant I would control what areas we would search. My job was to watch my dog for any indications that she had picked up the airborne scent particles wafting from my cat. Her job was to detect the scent, pinpoint the source, and take me there.

I started Rachel out in the wrong direction. This would ensure that she worked for a sufficient length of time before we came across Yogi's scent. On actual search missions, we might search for two hours before we came across the scent we were supposed to be looking for. I was teaching Rachel search dog "stick-to-it-iveness."

"Check this," I told her in each area as we worked through the woods around the cabin. Wherever I pointed my finger, Rachel would sniff for scent. She was trained to systematically search an area one section at a time, under my direction, until she hit on the scent.

As we covered more ground, I let Rachel reel out farther from me, knowing she was gaining confidence, as was I, as she searched. We were still thirty yards from Yogi when Rachel located the scent cone. Her body language dramatically showed she had detected what she was looking for—her head was elevated high as she strained to reach the scent hovering just out of reach. Her tail flagged back and forth as she intently zigged and then zagged within the fringes of the cone, honing in on the source. She dragged me straight up to the hidden crate. After standing and acknowledging Yogi with evident excitement, Rachel ran back joyfully to tell me she'd found her quarry. She jumped up on me—her trained signal that she had made a find.

"Show me!" I commanded. Rachel half wiggled, half ran her way back to Yogi. It was time for the cheese, and she knew it.

Rachel found Yogi three times that day, hidden in three different locations around my cabin, with me giving her more free rein to search each time. She had easily proved she understood that I wanted her to find a concealed cat. It was time to see if she could find one particular cat in a sea of other cat scents. That would be a much harder task, but my "retired" search dog had proven that she deserved a chance.

"Can I borrow your cats—and your house—for an afternoon?"

It was a good thing that Jeanne Mason was a close friend. Even so, I'm pretty sure she thought I was crazy. "I want to test Rachel on something more challenging," I explained. Jeanne laughed and told me I could come whenever I wanted and give it a shot.

The next day, I pulled up to her house with Rachel in the back of the truck and parked out front. The house was a big contemporary model on a cul-de-sac with lots of places to search and hide, but that wasn't why I'd picked it. Jeanne's personal menagerie included five cats, three dogs, and a bird—and lots of scents to throw an eager search dog off track. I knew

Rachel could find Yogi on command, but I needed to see if she could scent discriminate and tell one cat from another—or if she'd think that a cat was a cat was a cat. I figured this would be a good test for her, with lots of distractions.

Jeanne had already settled all three dogs outside when I got there. Their scents would be all over the house, but the dogs themselves wouldn't be present to distract Rachel. All five cats, though, had the run of the place. I went inside and Jeanne scooped up Kohala, a fat, shorthaired calico and the biggest and bravest of her cats, to serve as Rachel's target. I took a sterile gauze pad from my search vest, tore it open, and removed it from its protective paper. I rubbed the gauze pad around Kohala's mouth, ears, and back, then stuffed it inside a plastic bag for safe keeping until I was ready to use it.

Jeanne put Kohala in a crate and hid him in the master bedroom, under her bed. I went outside and harnessed Rachel, not sure what to expect from her when I brought her inside. Rachel had never been to the house before, but she was most definitely happy to see Jeanne anywhere. She nuzzled up for a good scratch between the shoulder blades before getting started.

As soon as I scented Rachel on the gauze pad, all socializing was over. She was focused on the smell of Kohala as we worked through the house. Rachel was on a long lead so I could control her from room to room.

"Check this," I commanded as I pointed in and under various cubbyholes and potential kitty caves. We made our way through the kitchen, checking cupboards, drawers, and a food pantry. Rachel did a great job of ignoring tempting food items and seemed to understand the mission at hand. We descended into the den where the first test of the day loomed—the bird. Rachel jumped up to sniff the angry, squawking lime green lovebird and nearly knocked the dangling birdcage to the ground. Jeanne warned me to be careful—the tiny bird had a mean streak and would likely hurt my dog should it escape its cage.

"Leave it!" I commanded. Thankfully, Rachel didn't try to befriend the angry bird. She immediately put her nose back down and carried on sniffing.

We continued searching the den, checking under a love seat and behind a desk. Then Rachel encountered her first cat. It was Miska, a longhaired solid gray cat who hunched up and hissed at her. Rachel sniffed from a distance and seemed grateful to be told to leave that cat alone.

The next cat was sleeping on the couch in the living room. This one was Princess, a white puffball of a cat who seemed indifferent to the presence of my dog. In fact, she only slightly cracked open her eyes to sneak a peek at my dog and quickly closed them, returning to her all-important catnap. Rachel trotted up, sniffed the cat, and then trotted on. My hopes that she could differentiate between pets skyrocketed.

We worked through the dining room and family room, as I continually found places to point out and command "check this." Then we started down a long hall that led to the bedrooms. Rachel seemed to catch the scent she was looking for as she first entered the hallway, but I wanted her to search the entire house. I anchored her with the leash and moved through the first, empty bedroom, and into the second one. There, nestled in the crevice between two pillows, was Porsche, a plump, smoky gray cat. He glared at us but never made a sound. Rachel gave him a quick sniff and turned around to leave—proof positive that she knew this kitty was not the one she was looking for.

"Good giiirrrl," I encouraged her. "Where's the kitty?"

As we made our way into Jeanne's bedroom, I let the leash out. Rachel knew exactly where she was going and what she was doing. With her head down and tail waving high, she dove under the bed to find the crated cat. She was bowing like she used to do as a puppy—her head was under the bed and her haunches up in the air, tail wiggling with delight. I remained quiet to see if she would come and signal me that she had found her target. Moments later, after she had finished introducing herself to Kohala, she backed out, turned around, ran back, and jumped up on me. There was no doubt that Rachel knew she'd found the right cat. I was ecstatic. Rachel and I were one step closer to being in business as pet detectives.

In finding Kohala, Rachel showed me she could tell one cat apart in a houseful of them—all the proof I needed that each cat has its own individual scent. I was delighted with Rachel's success, but I still needed to know if she could do the same for a dog—a member of her own species. More challenging yet, I needed to know if she could follow a trail made by a pet, as opposed to conducting an area search. If we were going to find lost animals, we would not have the luxury of a closed perimeter on every case. Rachel needed to be able to trail the scent of a dog, and, because we had focused on cadaver detection and I had spent only a limited amount of time in training her to follow a scent trail, I had my doubts about whether she'd be able to do that.

In December 1996, just two weeks after the cat-finding exercise at Jeanne's house, Rachel got her big chance. I had taken Rachel along on one of my monthly bloodhound training exercises in Livermore, California. Jeanne and I had arranged to meet with a fellow police bloodhound handler Jeff Schettler, his wife Judy, and their bloodhound Ronin. Jeff was a police officer for the city of Alameda and lived in Livermore, an hour north of Santa Cruz and east of the city of Oakland. Months earlier, Jeff had contacted me and asked if I could help him train his bloodhound puppy. I agreed and we began training on a weekly basis. Jeff ultimately became a leading authority on training bloodhounds. His memoir, *Red Dog Rising,* chronicles his amazing work with his bloodhound Ronin.

Jeanne and I met Jeff and Judy in the parking lot of an abandoned building in an industrial section of Livermore. Jeanne brought Kea, and I had both A.J. and Rachel with me. We all arrived around 8:30 in the morning.

Our preference was to train early when the scent was lowest to the ground. Heat causes scent to rise, often above the level of the dog's nose, while the coolness of the evening and moisture will cause scent to drop down and hover close to the ground. In addition, heat will "burn out" a search dog and create rapid fatigue. In the past, I have been able to work my bloodhounds for hours in cold weather but have worked cases in the baking heat of a summer day where my dogs were useless and stopped working after just twenty minutes. But the level of tenacity of a search dog to work in miserably hot weather varied from dog to dog and probably depended upon whether or not the handler was willing to extensively train his or her dog in the heat. That would explain the wimpy nature of my spoiled-rotten dogs who, like me, melted like putty when the thermometer registered anything over ninety degrees.

The training method that Jeanne, Jeff, and I used to train our dogs is known as "urban man trailing," and it is, by far, the most challenging. My dogs had had a taste of it during their early lessons at bloodhound training camps, but my friends and I were able to raise it to a more complicated level because there were just five of us, and we were all experienced handlers with experienced dogs. With this method, we purposely trained our dogs in areas where there were plenty of distractions. Cars, pedestrians, animals, and an unlimited number of scents in an urban area provide an assault on a dog's sense of smell. Only the smartest and most disciplined trailing dogs are able to pick up a scent in that kind of environment and follow it until they find the source.

Rachel's task that day would be more complex than anything she and I had done so far in our pet-finding work. Instead of searching from one limited area to the next for an item like a cat, she was going to start at the beginning of a scent trail and retrace the path of scent left by a "victim"—in this case a four-footed victim named Ronin. If she did it right, she'd follow Ronin's route and wind up positively identifying him.

But before I could work Rachel, we needed to work the other dogs first. Jeff worked Ronin, I worked A.J., and then Jeanne finished up with Kea. Everyone was hot and tired. I knew everyone would have been happy if we had ended the training session then and there. But my friends knew, even if they didn't really approve, that I intended to work Rachel, too. I went over to Jeff's truck and collected scent from Ronin. I told Jeff, Judy, and Jeanne where I wanted them to stand in the parking lot and what I needed them to do.

I brought Rachel out of her wire crate, put the search harness on her, and got ready to head out. To prove to myself that Rachel knew what she was doing, I needed her to choose Ronin from a "scent lineup" of dogs when we returned. I asked Jeff, Judy, and Jeanne to spread out across the parking lot with each holding one of the dogs on a lead. I wanted Ronin to be farthest from Rachel, so that she'd have to pass up the other two dogs, A.J. and Kea, to choose Ronin from the pack. I suspected my friends thought that the purpose of my unorthodox training exercise was silly, but I didn't care. I had to know if it could be done.

I scented Rachel on Ronin's gauze pad. She immediately took off working the search. I could tell by the way she was pulling in the harness that she was on the scent. Her body language was very different from that of the bloodhounds. A.J. worked with his nose rather high and he had a goofy on-the-scent pace that could best be described as a camel waddle. Chase looked like the classic bloodhound and worked with her nose directly on the ground. But Rachel held her nose at mid-level, pointed out and not down. She leaned forward in the harness with her weight on her front shoulders, kind of like a dog pulling a sled. I had watched Ronin jog this same trail when he tracked Judy an hour earlier, thus I had a general idea of where the hound's scent was located.

In places where Ronin had overshot Judy's trail and then come back to pick it up again, Rachel overshot as well. She was working it beautifully—first south down the uneven sidewalk with weeds popping up between the cracks. Then she worked across an intersection, vacant of traffic, and west along a fairly busy street with an occupied manufacturing business and a parking lot full of cars owned by people busy working inside.

When she ran out of scent going west, Rachel turned slightly north to stay on Ronin's trail. We came to a spot where Judy had spent much of her morning waiting for all the dogs to find her. Rachel ignored the giant pool of invisible human scent created by Judy's remaining stationary for hours. This confirmed for me that Rachel was working a scent other than Judy's.

I was thrilled to see that Rachel was doing so well. I praised her as we jogged along. But I knew that the biggest test was yet to come. Four people and two dogs in our party had walked or jogged that same route earlier that morning. Although I hoped she had locked onto Ronin's scent when I first presented it under her nose, I had no way of knowing for sure just who Rachel was currently trailing. But I was about to find out.

As we made the final turn that took us back to the staging area, I could see the six of them lined up like bowling pins: Kea, the golden retriever, sitting next to Jeanne; my A.J. standing next to Judy; and Ronin, Jeff's bloodhound, sitting next to Jeff at the very end of the line.

Rachel didn't even glance at the other dogs. I dropped the lead and let it drag on the ground behind her. That way, I would not influence her decision and she would, hopefully, demonstrate that she was only looking for Ronin. Rachel ran past Kea, then A.J., and loped straight up to Ronin. After wiggling around and returning the friendly greeting that the handsome hound extended to her, Rachel raced back and jumped up on me.

"Show me!" I cried. Rachel made her way back to Ronin, happily wiggling and dipping and nudging him to play. "Good Girl!" I exclaimed.

Once I said the familiar praise words, Rachel dropped Ronin like a rotten rawhide. She locked her eyes on me in anticipation of a cheddar moment. Impatiently, she jumped up on me and began scratching at my vest, drooling and barking for me to cough up the goods. Under any other circumstances, my normally obedient dog wouldn't have been allowed to act that way. But Rachel knew that the end of a successful search was a no-holds-barred celebration of jumping up, barking, and generally acting like a crazy dog. I dug into the pocket of my vest and gave Rachel her cubes of praise.

My friends were impressed in spite of themselves. "She's a really great search dog," Jeanne announced. She then echoed a question, a statement, really, that I had heard seven months prior, back when I first proposed my idea to train a dog to track lost pets to my peers. "Are you *sure* you want to waste her talent on searching for lost pets?" Jeanne knew what I knew about the fickle nature of the law enforcement and search dog communities. Making the transition from respected police officer with proven search dogs to the laughable occupation of "pet detective" would likely elicit teasing, smirks, and total rejection from my peers.

I was beyond sure. And frankly, I didn't really care what others thought. Rachel and I were on the verge of pioneering a whole new way of searching for lost pets. My dog had proved, in training at least, that she could find lost cats and dogs. And I could hardly wait to let her try the real thing.

Chapter Eight
A DIAMOND IN THE ROUGH

Rachel's very first search was a success, although it involved a sad ending. My vet's office called to say that a client's cat named Pearl was injured and missing. Pearl's owner watched in horror as a car backed over Pearl. Her cat let out a horrendous scream and was last seen running towards a deck at the side of her home. Within five minutes, Rachel found Pearl, deceased underneath that same deck. The very next day, we responded on another missing cat case. In a strange twist of fate, Rachel found that cat deceased, also underneath a deck. It was a sobering start to our pet-tracking career.

Fully confident in Rachel's ability to find lost pets, I posted a flyer in my veterinarian's office and waited for even more cases. I was busy with my job at UCSC and ongoing work with my bloodhounds, but I was anxious to add pet searches with Rachel to my schedule. It was only a matter of days before I received my next call.

Diamond, a thirteen-year-old black Doberman, was missing from her home in San Jose. Her owner, Marie Martinez, had been searching for her dog for six days, hearing from people in the neighborhood that they had seen the Doberman. Unfortunately, these witnesses never called quickly enough for Marie to catch up. Trying to track the shadow of her beloved dog was frightening and frustrating for Marie, and in desperation, she had come to the same conclusion that I had when A.J. was lost: What she needed was a search dog. Marie e-mailed a group of bloodhound owners looking for a dog to track Diamond, and since word was out among my fellow handlers that I was taking on this unconventional new role with one of my dogs, she was quickly referred to me.

Despite the long period of time that had elapsed between Diamond's disappearance and the call from her owner, I took Rachel to Marie's house to see if we could help. Marie, a slim woman in her early thirties, met us at the door. Her job involved training and showing horses. She was a gutsy woman who could haul a horse trailer over an icy roadway or attempt to ride a fractious, bucking horse without fear. Yet, just as A.J.'s disappearance had caused me to unravel, Marie had a pale, frantic look on her face.

"Diamond is like a child to me," Marie said as soon as I was in her front door. "I keep hearing from people who've seen her this week that she's still alive. I *have* to get her back." I asked if Marie had any pictures of her dog, and the reply seemed to confirm Diamond's status in the household: The Doberman had her own photo album, complete with puppy pictures, photos of Diamond in Halloween costumes, Diamond with a birthday cake, Diamond at a horse show, and Diamond posing with family members.

As I listened to Marie talk about her dog, I was struck by how much these lost pet cases were similar to the missing-person investigations I had worked. I'm not sure what I'd expected on these kinds of calls, but it wasn't the exact same pit-of-my-stomach, God-I-hope-this-missing-family-member-is-OK sensation I'd had when I searched for lost people as a police officer. If anything, this was even *more* personal, probably because I had lived through the same fear when I'd lost my own dog. But there was one glaring difference between pet searches verses lost person searches—there were no barriers between me and this woman who had asked for my help.

On a lost-person investigation, I seldom spoke with the family members. A patrol officer or detective was always assigned to interview and communicate with the family of the lost person. That made it easy and convenient for me to be emotionally unattached. But Marie was going to be right at my side for as long as this took, and there were no other officers here to take over where I left off after picking up scent material. For better or worse, we were getting to know each other very quickly and intimately. The same nervousness, desperation, and grief I had seen on cases of missing persons were present in Marie's alternately wistful and determined speech, in the tension of her movements as she struggled to keep her composure while talking about her missing dog, and in the way she slipped tenses as she talked about Diamond's daily routine.

Using a sterile gauze pad, I wiped Diamond's blanket to collect her scent. Then I turned to Rachel, who waited eagerly in her search vest, placed the gauze under her nose, and commanded her, "Take scent."

Rachel took off immediately, working her way around the yard, then trotting a pattern through the neighborhood—over several front lawns, along the landscaping, in the center of the roadway, and on sidewalks. We navigated around a few rose gardens and through a weed-filled vacant lot, past yards with thick hedges, cars parked in driveways and mailboxes. Rachel sniffed up to a few porches, then continued to the play yard of a nearby school. I was amazed, as I had been on the day Kea had tracked A.J. through the woods, at how different a dog's trail is from that of a person. I could almost picture the black Doberman from the photos going about her rounds in the neighborhood, stopping to smell all the places where other people's pets had made their mark, taking in all the scents on her regular route. At the school, Marie confirmed that Diamond had been spotted there three days before by a teacher who lived down the street.

Rachel then led us across the street and into another neighborhood. Marie carried pink flyers with a photo of Diamond, passing them out to everyone we passed as Rachel worked the scent.

"Have you seen my dog?" Marie asked each person we encountered along the trail. She even convinced a group of five young boys on bicycles to start searching for Diamond.

"I did see her," answered one woman at a nearby park, "but that was a couple days ago. I have no idea where she went from here."

We were glad to hear about the sighting, but the fact that we were working days behind Diamond continued to be discouraging. I knew full well that a large dog like that could travel miles each day.

After several hours of searching on foot, I had to tell Marie that we had done all we could do. It was getting dark, and I had told her up front that we would be at a tremendous disadvantage trying to search for a dog that had already been missing for so long. I wasn't surprised when she didn't take it well, and I wished there were more I could do for her.

"Can't we please keep going?" Marie asked. "You know Rachel is following her scent. If we just keep at it, she might catch up with her."

I thought of the day A.J. had disappeared, and of how Kea had been on his scent within less than an hour of his escape. And then there were the missing person searches I had conducted. A team of officers and volunteers would set up a perimeter immediately upon discovering the person was missing. Armed with handheld radios, maps, and a search plan, we would work the entire area, inch by inch, until we could either find the missing person or rule out the area. Marie had no team—just me and Rachel, and I knew that when we got back in my truck, she would be on her own again.

We had given it the better part of our day, and Rachel was glancing back at me frequently now, giving a very rare indication that she, too, was getting tired and needed to stop. "I'm really sorry," I answered Marie, as we came back by the schoolyard again and turned back toward her house. "I hope you'll find Diamond, and I wish I could do more, but we have exhausted our leads here. My best advice is that you not give up. Half your neighborhood already knows you are looking for your dog—make sure the other half knows, too."

Six months later, I ran into a Marie at a dog-related event in San Jose. She lit up when she saw me and ran over to announce her great news: She had found her dog. Marie had persisted in posting flyers and aggressively continued searching for Diamond. It was a just reward when the person who spotted a skinny black Dobie in a field had seen one of those posters. Marie had received the thing anyone who has lost a person or pet wants most: a happy reunion.

I was disappointed that Rachel hadn't found Diamond, but after years of training and experience in searching for people, I wasn't surprised. Any search-and-rescue dog handler can tell you that the number of cases with finds, especially with happy-ending finds, are in the small minority. It doesn't change the work we do, though. I was thrilled to learn that Marie had found her dog. It was her persistence that had done the job, and involving Rachel and me was one of the many ways she had demonstrated how determined she was to succeed.

Three weeks after the Diamond case, Rachel and I received another call from a distraught pet owner. I had worked a ten-hour graveyard shift at UCSC and arrived home exhausted. I had only been asleep for an hour when, at 9 A.M., my pager went off.

"I received a page from this number," I said wearily when I returned the call a few minutes later, hoping it was something worth being awakened for.

"My name is Robyn Yoslow," the woman on the line told me, "and my cat is missing. I was told that you have a dog that searches for missing pets."

I wanted very, very much to go back to bed, but Robyn continued, "His name is Mr. Bear, and we've had him for thirteen years. He can't possibly take care of himself. We have to find him before he gets hurt."

As much as I wanted to sleep, I couldn't refuse to help her. Anyone who gave a pet a name like "Mr. Bear" was going to be hard to turn down.

"I've only had an hour of sleep," I told Robyn. "And I have to go in early tonight to work a fourteen-hour shift."

"I'm so sorry," Robyn said, "but we really need your help. We will pay you. What's your fee?"

I explained that as I didn't have a business license, I would not be charging any fee at all. I'd be grateful, though, for a sandwich and a strong cup of coffee.

Robyn readily agreed, and I dragged myself out of bed, took a quick shower, and called Rachel off the couch so we could get to work. For her part, Rachel had not only enjoyed a good night's sleep, but a nice morning nap during my hour-long "night's sleep." She literally danced around me as I, feeling like I was in a fog, loaded our gear in the truck.

Despite her enthusiasm and my resolve, Rachel and I did not find Mr. Bear that day. In fact, Robyn and her husband, Mark, never found out what happened to him. The couple lived in an area where coyotes were common, and they were realistic enough to assume the worst when Rachel was unable to turn up any sign of their cat.

Even though I was unable to help them, the Yoslows seemed very grateful for my efforts and impressed to see Rachel tracking along on their cat's favorite haunts. They invited me to sit with them at their kitchen table. As promised, Robyn made me a great sandwich and a strong cup of coffee, while Mark offered some unsolicited but wise advice.

"You should start a business," Mark told me. "And you need to start charging a fee for your services." Both Mark and Robyn were savvy businesspeople, and I think they were amazed that I would actually drag myself out of bed on an hour's sleep and travel to their home to look for their lost cat—for no fee. I was still viewing my pet detective work as an experiment, but Mark saw it in a different light. As I retreated to my truck, he gave this parting advice: "You have a service that pet owners need and will gladly pay for."

I guess that was what I needed to hear. The following week, I filed my business name statement. I called my pet detective business "Pet Pursuit." On my business cards was the Pet Pursuit logo of a bloodhound with nose to the ground, following a set of dog prints. I even put magnetic pet detective signs with my phone number on my truck doors.

So far, Rachel and I had only found pets who were deceased or who were hidden during training, rather than truly lost, and it was clear from our first outings on real cases that we still had a lot to learn about lost pets. I felt assured, though, as I admired my new logo, that the combination of Rachel's search skills, my training in solving investigations, and my knowledge of missing persons search strategies and procedures would be enough to make our work successful.

I distributed flyers and business cards to area pet stores, veterinarians, and grooming shops to let them know about my services. Feeling that the local animal shelter would be an important place to advertise lost-pet services, I hand-delivered a stack of flyers and business cards to the front desk of the Santa Cruz SPCA. After all, the first place most pet owners go when their pet is missing is the shelter, and I was becoming increasingly aware of how important a quick response could be. Placing flyers at the SPCA lost-and-found counter was the best means to reach the pet owners who would most need my services. Best of all, if I could help families recover their missing pets *before* they had a chance of ending up in the animal shelter, I'd be helping the shelters, too. But instead of the support I had anticipated, I ran into the first roadblock in my new endeavor.

"I'm sorry," the shelter employee told me. "Since you have a for-profit business, we can't allow you to advertise your services here." I was disappointed, but there was nothing I could do about the policy, so I took the flyers home.

Despite the lack of advertising, the cases kept coming in. Rachel and I were soon working the trail of a dog who had gotten himself in trouble chasing a cat. While in hot pursuit, Sky, a three-year-old husky, had been hit by a car. Sky's owner, Mike Shook, a machinist at a nearby shop, had witnessed the accident and watched in horror as Sky took off running down a nearby railroad track after he was hit. Mike chased after Sky but lost sight of him heading east across Highway 9 and into the redwood forest of Henry Cowell State Park. The accident happened at 6:00 P.M. and Mike searched the forest in vain for nearly five hours. Mike got my phone number from a local veterinarian and called me the following morning.

I immediately responded with Rachel. A light rain began to fall as I went to meet with Mike. Like pretty much anything else to do with water, Rachel hated the rain. Many people think that rain will destroy scent or that it some how makes it difficult for a dog to work a scent trail. But rain actually *enhances* scent particles, making them easier to detect. That is why some objects that seemingly have no odor, like an asphalt roadway or the family dog, are suddenly detected by human olfactory sensors when they become wet. I would much rather work my search dogs in wet weather than in dry or hot weather. The only exception to this was Rachel and her wimpy hesitation to even step off my redwood deck to pee during a rainstorm. I said a quick prayer that my dog would focus on Sky's scent and not get distracted by the weather.

I pulled up outside the machine shop where Mike worked. Sky went to work with Mike every day. I could tell this dog was loved. Sky had a fleece bed in the corner of the shop, and he was considered something of a mascot for the place, greeting customers and keeping them company while they waited for service. The shop owner was worried sick about Sky, too. He agreed to assist in the search by driving his car along behind Mike and me as we worked Rachel.

The steady rain had tapered off to a light drizzle by the time I took Rachel from the truck. She began to wiggle her tail in excitement at meeting these new people and getting ready to work as I snapped her harness in place. Mike gave me the bed with Sky's scent, and Rachel strained forward in her harness toward it. I had Rachel sit and placed the fleece bedding under her nose.

"Take scent!" I commanded. As usual, Rachel had cheated. She had already detected the airborne scent particles lofting off the bedding before I officially presented it to her. Sometimes Rachel snuffled the scent article, giving it several deep whiffs before she headed out on the trail, while other times she gave a simple, single sniff. This probably had something to do with the direction the wind was blowing at the time I brought out the scent article. If Rachel was standing in the scent cone and was able to pick up the airborne scent from the scent article before I gave her the "take scent" command, she only gave a single sniff before she moved out. But if there was no breeze or Rachel was standing upwind from the scent article, then she would inhale the scent article several times before taking off.

In this instance, Rachel gave the bedding a token sniff and we were off in a flash. She headed north along the railroad tracks and then cut east toward Highway 9, a busy two-lane highway that snakes its way through the Santa Cruz Mountains. Mike had spent the evening before searching the thickly forested area on the east side of the highway. He had last seen Sky heading into that area. It was the most likely place to find the dog and exactly where Rachel was leading us.

"That's the direction that I last saw him running!" Mike yelled as he jogged behind us. Rachel proceeded to work two blocks through Harvey West Park, an industrial area that bordered the redwood forest, until she reached the edge of Highway 9. I pulled her back and waited for traffic to clear.

"Get to work," I instructed Rachel as I released my tight grip on the lead.

She proceeded east across the wet highway and headed down the embankment into the redwood forest. Under the thick canopy of the redwood trees, Rachel began to work a series of dirt trails throughout the woods. She covered the entire area that Mike had searched the night before. She worked down several trails for a short distance, and then retraced her steps. That was an indication that the scent did not continue on these trails. For the next fifteen minutes, Rachel circled the wooded area, tracing many of the same places she had already worked. But she did not branch out or commit to any trail that would lead deeper into the woods.

Then she worked up the embankment to the east edge of Highway 9. She stopped and looked across the roadway. We were now about an eighth of a mile north of the industrial area where we had originally entered the woods. When traffic was clear, I allowed Rachel to move forward. She crossed back over the highway, heading west, and worked up an embankment on the far side. There were two linemen working on a pipe. Rachel ignored them and continued to work, a clear indication that she was still following Sky's scent.

"We're looking for a lost husky," I announced to the workmen who were staring at Rachel's bright orange "Search Dog" vest.

"You're kidding," one of the workmen said in disbelief. "Your dog can do that?"

"Have you seen my dog?" Mike interrupted.

"No," the workman said. "Sorry."

"If you see him," Mike said, "please let me know. I work down at the machine shop by Harvey West Park."

We continued following Rachel as she climbed up a steep embankment heading back toward the railroad tracks. Once on the tracks, Rachel was committed to heading north. As she continued to work the scent, I gave Mike my assessment.

"She's definitely on Sky's scent," I told him. "Remember how she was working in the woods back there? How she would not commit to any direction but kept backing off of it?"

He nodded. I was glad that Rachel's body language was so easy to read.

"Do you see the difference?" I asked. "Now she's pulling in the harness, trotting at an even pace with her head held level. If she didn't have Sky's scent, she would be circling around here and cutting down these side paths to check for the scent. She's on it."

Rachel worked north along the tracks. The wet weather enhanced the pungent petroleum-based creosote from the damp railroad ties. Ignoring the olfactory assault as best she could, Rachel continued working the scent trail along the tracks for approximately two miles until she stopped at a train trestle suspended over a magnificent canyon. And there, my heroic dog would not budge. She could have easily put a paw through the open trestle boards suspended high above the canyon. But Rachel was too smart to try to cross. She looked up at me, her long pink tongue lolling out of her mouth, with a doggy grin on her face that seemed to say, "Okay Mom, I'm done."

According to his owner, the dog we were seeking was equally sensible.

"There is no way," Mike said, "no way Sky would cross that trestle."

"Neither will Rachel," I responded. "Let's see if there's a way around it."

On the west side of the tracks, a footpath snaked down through the canyon. Perhaps Sky had gone that way. I led Rachel off the trestle and down the path. But she lost interest and did not pick up the scent. It seemed we had come to the end of this trail. We had followed Sky's path for nearly three miles, and we had given Mike a pretty clear picture of the route his dog had taken.

"I'm sorry, but I'm going to have to leave soon," I told Mike. I had another two hours before I had to head into work. "Rachel is indicating that Sky was here on the railroad tracks. He probably cut off into the woods near here."

"What should I do now?" Sky's owner asked.

"Focus your search in the woods by these tracks," I answered. "Chances are, he's here somewhere. His injury will slow him down and give you a better chance of catching up with him. Make up some flyers and hand them out near here, and offer a reward. Notify the park rangers at the Pogonip and Henry Cowell parks and leave a flyer with them. If you find Sky, please be sure to call me."

I wished I had been called immediately after the car hit Sky, while he was still close. The most I could do was to follow the scent trail and give Mike a good idea of Sky's direction of travel. I left reluctantly for work, hoping the best for Mike and Sky.

Later that night, I received a call from Mike.

"I just wanted to let you know that Sky is home," he said. "I did as you suggested and focused my search in that area. Five hours after you left, I was on the railroad tracks looking for Sky and he came out of the woods."

"I can't thank you enough," he continued. "I would have been looking for Sky miles from where I found him if it hadn't been for you and your dog."

Unfortunately, in some cases even the best efforts of my dog and me couldn't help save a lost pet. That was certainly the story in our next case, one of the most frustrating and disappointing of them all.

By this time I was assigning each case a number, and this one was case 97-018. I drove just sixty miles to get there, but when I arrived, I found myself in completely unfamiliar territory, and, despite the fact that I had been asked to come, unwelcoming circumstances. One mansion followed another as I kept to the directions I had taken down over the phone. They were set acres apart on the open California coastal plains. These were million-dollar properties, but they were dotted across the flat landscape like so many haystacks in a field—no trees, no hills, nothing at all to break up the monotony.

Not a lot of places out here for a lost dog to disappear to, I thought as I pulled up the cobblestone driveway, put the truck in park, and reviewed my notes.

— "Toby" —fourteen-year-old, blind, deaf Norwich terrier

—Squeezed through gate three days ago, hasn't been seen since

—Owner, Pam Billings, thinks dog's been kidnapped by neighbors

—Owner going to consult with an animal psychic

I hopped out and walked to the back of the truck to check on Rachel, who was eagerly waiting for me to put her to work. "Doesn't seem like she'd need a psychic *and* a search dog, does it?" I asked her. She cocked her head and wagged her stubby tail, waiting to get started, oblivious to the apparent lack of confidence our new client had in our abilities.

I headed up the walk and rang the bell. A thin, middle-aged woman wearing pressed jeans, cowboy boots, and a cashmere sweater yanked open the door. She wore rings on almost every finger and a thin chain with a charm in the shape of a terrier around her neck. Her eyes were bloodshot, and her face puffy. I smelled alcohol from several feet away.

"I know just where you need to look," Pam slurred, sounding dejected, desperate, and way too bossy for this to start well. "The psychic told me." What followed that afternoon could serve as an example for writing a book about how *not* to search for a lost pet. Pam informed me that her psychic could visualize the little terrier caught by his leash in a stand of low brush in a field. Teetering unsteadily in her shiny, heeled boots, she wanted to head for a nearby field as soon as I rang the bell.

She'll break her neck if I take her with me, was my first thought, followed by a quick assessment of what it was going to take for me to gain control of this situation.

I reminded Pam as tactfully as possible that I was the pet detective and that I would conduct the search based upon my knowledge and experience.

I started by closing the front gate to confine Rachel within Toby's fenced yard. Using Toby's blanket as a scent article, I presented the scent to Rachel and gave the search command. She quickly searched the front, back, and side yards, and I made sure that we checked all potential hiding areas and places where a small dog could have become trapped. When Rachel did not show interest in any particular area, I was satisfied that Toby was not in the yard.

"Now le's go to the fields," Pam slurred with impatience.

"Now, we'll work a scent trail from the gate where Toby escaped," I countered.

And so it went. Following a clear scent trail, Rachel indicated that Toby was trapped in a wide pipe near an opening a quarter mile from Pam's house. The pipe was part of a labyrinth-like drainage system that crisscrossed under the ritzy homes in the area. And as if Rachel's "word" weren't enough evidence, there were feces from a small dog just inside the pipe, confirming in my mind that Toby was somewhere inside the maze of tubing.

I told Pam she should call a plumber to come out and investigate the pipe system. Continuing to follow her clairvoyant's advice and her drunken intuition, she insisted that would be a waste of time. When I pointed out the still-stinky evidence just inside the irrigation system, Pam shook her head and said it must be from a fox. She told me again to turn my attention to the fields, where her dog was surely languishing on his leash, waiting to be rescued. I obliged, but soon turned my attention to getting Rachel and myself out of there. I was so frustrated with this woman who refused to listen to reason and try to help her trapped dog that I couldn't get away from her fast enough.

Even though I believe he could have been brought home, Toby was never found. There were limits to what my knowledge, Rachel's skills, and our work together could accomplish, and with no authority to force my investigation as I would have in police work, I had no choice but to go home and toss and turn that night, thinking about the little dog I might have saved.

Most people who hear my pet detective saga want to know the same thing about these searches.

Why would you keep going out to search for pets you don't find, or worse yet, for pets you find dead?

My feelings about it then and now go back to a very simple principle that struck me again and again as I worked cases of missing persons and cases of missing pets. Life does not always provide a storybook ending. And in police work, especially, I often saw a seedy and sad side of life that the average citizen does not see. In search-and-rescue work, I was accustomed to working lost-person cases where the person was never found or was found deceased. Just like veterinary medicine mirrors medical treatment for people, I began to notice that my lost-pet investigations were all too like my lost-person searches.

But the biggest similarity of all was that in the most basic sense, love is love. Whether you feel it toward your eighty-year-old grandmother, your naughty twelve-year-old son, the cocker spaniel who trots up and presents you with your chewed-to-the-sole leather loafers, or the kitten who curls on your lap and purrs the evening away, it is the same emotion.

People who lose the pets they love need to have the best possible shot at getting their loved ones back safe and sound. And if, God forbid, those lost pets are dead, then the people who love them should be able to know the truth so they can accept it and mourn. They need closure, and I always believed that if I could offer that with my services, then I was still doing something to help.

I wish I could report that every lost-pet investigation I worked on ended with a joyful reunion, but that was not the case. I worked countless investigations where people were tormented by grief when they could not find the pet they loved. There was the woman who sold two guitars and her '65 Mustang in order to have enough money to launch a media campaign to find her lost dog, the elderly man who fixed an extra bowl of dog food every night for six months "just in case" his lost dog were to wander back home, and the man who wanted to divorce his wife because he wasn't sure he could ever forgive her for accidentally letting their indoor-only cat outside.

I took my happy endings where I could find them, but in the meantime, Rachel and I worked steadfastly to get to the bottom of our cases and always be mindful of the love our clients felt for their missing pets. Even after all the cases that ended badly, it was enough to make me want to keep searching.

Chapter Nine
A TALE OF TWO TRAILS

When my pager went off, I was doing something I hadn't made time for in months: thinking about my personal life instead of my professional one. I was at a seminar for Christian singles in San Jose, scanning the room for men who looked like potential dates. Between my day job as a cop and moonlighting as a pet detective, time spent even thinking about dating was a novelty in those days.

I didn't think about it long, though, because the pager beeped and I ducked out of the auditorium to return the call on a pay phone (these were the days before cell phones). As busy as I was with both jobs, I never knew what to expect when I returned a page. It could be one of my colleagues at the police department, looking for coverage on one of my days off, or an officer from a nearby law enforcement agency calling to see if my bloodhounds and I might be able to trail a criminal or work a missing person's trail. Or it could be someone who had seen the flyer at my veterinarian's office or heard about my pet detective business through word of mouth, hoping I'd be able to find their lost pet.

The caller was a woman looking for her cat.

"My cat Pippi is missing," she began. "I hope you can help me. I'm afraid a coyote may have killed her."

My mind wandered back to the auditorium, where the promise of picking up my last-priority personal life remained. But then reality kicked in; I had better luck at finding lost pets than I had at finding eligible men. The coyote case began to look like a viable option.

"Why do you think your cat was taken by a coyote?" I asked, thinking that perhaps she was mistaken.

"She's been missing for two days now," the woman began. "The morning she disappeared, I found some fur on my front lawn. And there's a spot of what looks like blood in the street in front of my house."

"And what makes you think a coyote did it?" I wondered aloud, thinking that it certainly sounded like her cat had met an unfortunate fate, but the evidence didn't point to any particular predator.

"We hear coyotes howling at night," the woman continued. "The newspaper boy has seen one a few blocks over . . . and Pippi isn't the first cat to disappear from the neighborhood."

The evidence was convincing enough for me, but it put me in an unusual position. I wasn't sure what this caller wanted from me. It sounded like her theory about her cat's fate was probably right—but if it was, there was really not much I could do to help her.

"I don't know that there's anything a search dog can do for you," I began.

"Could you please just come out and look?" the caller asked, her voice beginning to sound like a plea.

"Do you have anything that has only Pippi's scent on it?" I asked, mentally running through my schedule for the next day and trying to decide what I'd have to cancel or change to make time for a search with Rachel.

She had to think about the question. "No, I don't think so. I've got a second cat named Muffin. They share everything. I don't think there's anything here with just Pippi's scent."

I told her that without an uncontaminated scent article, something with strictly Pippi's scent on it, working my dog would be pointless.

And then she began to cry. "I need to know if this is Pippi's blood," she said. "Can't you come and look at it? I'll pay you anything."

This was the first time I had been asked to evaluate physical evidence rather than to search for a lost pet. This case took place long before I incorporated more sophisticated forensic testing like blood analysis test kits and Luminol into my pet detective work. At the time, I wasn't sure how to proceed. I had some training in blood-spatter evidence, but I wasn't sure what I could determine just by looking at the stain. After a minute's deliberation, I decided that Rachel could tell me if the stain was blood, and that if this woman really wanted to pay me to come out and look at a dark stain in the road, I was willing to go.

"What's your name?" I asked, knowing that I'd never back down once I wrote down her name and address and began thinking of this as an open case.

Her name was Marilyn Maynard.

"I can't guarantee that I'll be able to help you, but I'm willing to try," I told her. "I charge $150 to come out and conduct a search—even if I don't find your cat."

"When can you get here?" was her reply.

The best I could do was the next afternoon, as it was already dark and I had to work the morning shift at UCSC. As soon as my shift was over, Rachel and I prepared to search for Pippi. I grabbed Rachel's harness, both of our orange work vests, my search pack, and a stash of the cubed cheese that would ensure Rachel knew how grateful I would be for her good work. I dropped the gate on the back of the truck, and Rachel leaped up and ducked into her crate, ready to go. We headed for the address Marilyn had given me on the outskirts of Aptos, a mountainous area just outside Santa Cruz. As I drove, I could see Rachel in the rearview mirror, peeking at me and no doubt wondering when on earth we were going to get started.

Marilyn's house was nestled in a quiet cul-de-sac in a housing tract at the base of some steep, rugged mountains. The neighborhood with neat lawns and flower gardens gave the illusion of civilized suburban life, but considering the wild terrain surrounding these homes, I was sure bobcats, coyotes, deer, and even a few mountain lions were the neighbors of the deceptively sedate community.

I left Rachel in her crate while I went to meet Marilyn.

A petite woman in her early fifties answered my knock. The dark circles under her eyes indicated she had not slept well. "I'm so glad you're here," she said. "Our second cat has disappeared, too. We let Muffin out last night, but she never came home. She's always at the door in the morning wanting to come in. She's eight hours overdue."

A casually dressed man, also in his fifties, walked up behind Marilyn and introduced himself as her husband, Clay. He had a warm handshake and an aura of kindness that made me feel at ease. It soon became clear that Marilyn wasn't the only one who loved these cats.

As I did on every case, I asked the owners if they had any photos of their cats that I could see. They had several, including a couple in frames. Pippi was a gray, fourteen-year-old tabby with white paws; Muffin a two-year-old longhaired calico. It was obvious as the couple talked about their cats and answered my questions about each cat's routine and habits that Pippi and Muffin were not just cats—they were family.

Along with the fear the couple felt that they would never see their cats again came the guilt they felt for putting their cats into harm's way. Marilyn acknowledged that letting her cats outdoors in coyote country was not an ideal living arrangement. She told me that she wished she could have kept them as indoor-only pets, but that both Pippi and Muffin had always found a way to convince their owners to let them out again. Muffin, in particular, would howl for hours nonstop at the back door until she was let outside. As I spoke with Marilyn and Clay, my plan for their case quickly changed from the original intent—to analyze the stain in the driveway and leave it at that—to figuring out a way to try to track two missing cats. I had to at least give it a try.

The first thing I needed to do was evaluate the saucer-sized stain on the asphalt in front of the house. Whatever it was, there were smaller, pea-sized droplets of it leading away from the cul-de-sac toward the steep wilderness area adjacent to the property. It was almost impossible for me to tell by just looking at it if it was blood. But Rachel would know.

After her years of work sniffing for evidence at crime scenes, there was no doubt Rachel would alert on the stain if it was decomposing human or animal blood if I asked her to. It was just a matter of giving her a different command than the "Search" command we had been using so much lately. I unloaded Rachel from the truck and allowed her to empty her bladder.

I opened my search pack and slipped on a pair of leather Franklin batting gloves to protect my hands. Other dog handlers normally used leather gardening gloves, but I loved my Franklins. They were thick enough to prevent injuries, such as blisters created by the sliding movement of the nylon tracking lead, yet thin enough that I could feel the slightest change in tension emanating from the pull in my dog's harness.

I snapped Rachel into her nylon tracking harness and put on her "Search Dog" vest. We were standing about ten yards from the stain. Rachel looked up at me, knowing that a search command would be coming her way any minute.

"Do you want to work?" I asked her. Rachel licked her lips, shifted her weight, and eagerly looked up at me. "You ready?"

"Find bones." It was a cadaver command I hadn't given Rachel in years, but she quickly demonstrated that she had not forgotten her training. We were downwind from the stain, and Rachel seemed to pick it up the minute I released her collar. She trotted directly up to the stain, sniffed the spot on the asphalt, scratched it with her paw, squatted, and urinated. The signal that had alerted me to evidence finds at crime scenes in the past hadn't been lost at all from lack of use. There was no mistaking Rachel's find. The stain was blood.

It seemed a reasonable assumption to work on that the blood belonged to Pippi. If that was the case, then I had "something" with her scent. But I was not absolutely *sure* that it was Pippi's blood and wished that I had a tuft of fur from Pippi's cat bed instead. I had worked cases before where the scent article used was *thought* to belong to the suspect, only to learn later that I was actually tracking the scent of a person who was not involved in the crime. The most critical element when working a scent discrimination-trailing-dog is having something that you *know* contains the scent you plan to track. I decided to take my chances and use the blood as scent material.

I gave Rachel a drink of water and told her to take a rest while I prepared to shift from cadaver to trailing mode. Rachel obediently flopped down on the lawn to await her next instruction, rolling in the cool grass.

Using a sterile gauze pad, I swiped the stain on the ground to collect the scent I hoped belonged to Pippi. I walked over to Rachel and asked if she was ready again. She abandoned her roll in the grass, jumped to her feet, shook off, and was ready in an instant. I snapped the lead into Rachel's nylon harness, brought the gauze pad up under her nose, and commanded, "Take scent. Search!"

Rachel immediately went to work. This time, we were attempting to follow the ground scent left behind by Pippi. Marilyn and Clay came along as I jogged behind Rachel.

We worked through the front yard, sometimes at a fast jog and other times at a slow walk, checking the bushes and areas where Pippi had sometimes taken catnaps. We searched the backyard bushes and some possible hiding spaces as well. Rachel was interested, but gave no alerts, busily sniffing her way from one area to the next.

We moved to the front yard again and continued to search. Rachel checked two more houses to the west and then turned herself around and worked back to Pippi's house. After fifteen minutes of this, it was clear that there was no fresh scent trail leading away from Pippi's house. This told me one of two things: either Pippi was still in the immediate area but we had failed to find her hiding place, or the three-day-old scent trail of a cat's body being carried away by a predator was too weak, in this case at least, for my dog to follow.

"I know the stain is blood, though I can't be sure it's Pippi's," I explained. "It seems likely though, because Rachel is telling me whatever creature that blood came from spent a lot of time in your yard." I paused a moment and reached down to stroke Rachel on the head before I stated the obvious. "Since Pippi disappeared right before you found it, I'm afraid it's probably her blood."

Marilyn nodded in agreement, solemn, but not surprised. She had hoped I would come and tell her the stain was something else—and find her lost cat, too. Instead, I had confirmed her worst fear.

She took a deep breath. "Can you do anything for Muffin?"

Suddenly we were back where we had started the night before on the phone. "Do you have anything with only Muffin's scent on it?" I asked, thinking that the answer would probably be no.

But this time, there was something. "I found a tuft of fur on the lawn that belongs to Muffin," Clay said helpfully. "It's got the same long orange and black calico hairs she does. I'm sure it's hers."

I told him to lead the way, then picked up the little clump of fur using a small plastic bag. I gave Rachel another break, and a tummy rub, and provided cool water and rest in the shade of a tree. The temperature was rising from the high seventies into the low eighties and Rachel felt it. She panted heavily. I gave her an extra five minutes to cool down while I sat next to her, hydrating myself with bottled water from my search pack. When I knew we were ready, I rose to my feet, as did my dog. I snapped the lead back onto the harness and put the open bag under Rachel's nose.

"Take scent," I commanded, as Rachel's wet nose wiggled from side to side. She immediately began to cast about the front yard, sniffing the same bushes she had checked when she had searched for Pippi. Rachel bypassed the houses on the west side, though, and began to work through the front yard to the east. We continued past the neighbors' houses she had searched when working the bloodstain scent and beelined north toward the entrance to the cul-de-sac.

This was clearly a different scent from the trail she had worked just ten minutes earlier. We worked at a faster pace, moving at a brisk jog. Rachel was pulling hard in the harness, a sign that she was working a fresh scent trail.

At the opening of the cul-de-sac, Rachel had three directions to choose from: the crossroad heading west, east, or the entrance to another subdivision that was straight ahead. We worked west first. Rachel pulled me about twenty yards before she slowed down, turned her head, and made eye contact with me. Eye contact meant no scent. I felt the familiar warmth of pride that my dog was so astute at her work. There was no chasing of ghost trails on this case. Rachel was hot on Muffin's scent. I knew I could trust her instincts.

And her instincts said Muffin had not traveled west. We turned around and headed east. We jogged past a woman walking with her two children and a golden retriever.

"Look at that dog, Mommy!" one of the children squealed as we ran past. "That's a search dog." Under normal circumstances, Rachel would have gone to pieces at the attention—wiggling her way over to the children to see if they might pet her and doing her best to make friends with the new dog.

But on this day she didn't even glance in their direction. She was on a fresh trail and even a parade of golden retrievers rolling down the street wouldn't have broken her concentration.

We continued heading east at a fast pace. Clay was able to keep up with me, but Marilyn began to fall behind. We worked about a block, continuing toward the steep, mountainous terrain of the state park—the likely home of the predators.

Suddenly, Rachel lifted her nose as she picked up an airborne scent. She cut north from the roadway and started to drag me up a steep embankment toward an open field. As I scrambled through an area littered with gravel, I slipped and dropped the lead to break the fall with my hands. I hit the ground hard and felt sharp pieces of gravel cut into my unprotected elbows. Rachel raced ahead without me, even faster with no pull on the leash to slow her down. She ran ahead into the field above me, casting back and forth in bird-dog fashion, tail wiggling with excitement, clearly narrowing in on a scent.

And then, to everyone's shock except Rachel's, a flash of black and orange calico came zipping out of the field. "Did you see her!?" Marilyn shouted.

"See who?" Clay asked, having missed seeing the cat make her hasty get away from my dog.

"Muffin!" Marilyn exclaimed. "Kat just flushed her out of that field! Right where Rachel is searching right now. She must have been hiding up here."

"Gooood girrrl," I gushed as I turned to praise Rachel, who was still above me. But Rachel was too busy to accept my praise and wasn't even thinking about cheddar cheese. She was sniffing something new in the field. Her excited bird-dog behavior suddenly shifted to a more serious search mode. The animated attitude she'd had as she raced along on the airborne live cat scent was gone. Rachel was now moving slowly, intently investigating something stationary on the ground. She sniffed, squatted and peed. Something was decomposing in the field.

I moved closer to see what she had found, with a certain sense of dread that I already knew what it was. Knowing how fragile she was, I instructed Marilyn to wait on the road and asked Clay to come to where Rachel was sniffing. Rachel was alerting on a small tuft of gray animal fur—it could have been gray tabby fur, it could have been Pippi's, but I couldn't tell. Clay also examined it and couldn't tell either.

The use of a forensic hair examination or a DNA test was still many searches away and did not occur to me. Instead, I relied on my investigative skills and my growing knowledge of lost-cat investigations to come up with the most likely scenario of what had happened to the gray cat. I surmised that a coyote had killed Pippi and carried her from the street to the field, a safe distance in the predator's mind from the hub of human activity below. Chances are, Muffin had done a bit of her own sleuthing to end up in the same location. Missing her friend and relying on her own keen sense of smell, she had probably followed her companion's scent to the field. Muffin would certainly not have been the first cat to do so. I had heard of several cases where one cat was missing from a household and a second cat had led a family member to it.

By the time Rachel and I got back to my truck, Muffin had reappeared at home and was slinking up the driveway, obviously wary of the dog in her territory. I gave Rachel a fistful of cubed cheddar cheese followed by a drink of water and loaded her into her crate. She curled around in a circle, settled into the coolness of the sheet-covered dog mattress, and let out a big sigh. She would be dozing within minutes.

With the threat of a strange dog out of the way, Muffin hustled to Marilyn, who picked her up, nuzzled her face in the cat's fur and burst into tears.

"You saved Muffin's life," she said. My thoughts swung abruptly from unadulterated pride in Rachel's excellent trailing work to empathy for Marilyn's emotions. As we talked, Marilyn wept and I put my arm around her. Then something happened that I had not expected. I found myself crying with Marilyn. In all my years as a 9-1-1 dispatcher, police officer, and cadaver dog handler, I had been exposed to many heart wrenching, tragic situations. Yet for the exception of the Polly Klaas search, I had never once shed a tear. The fact that I was crying with a woman whose cat had died struck me as odd, yet I sensed that God was doing something in my heart.

It suddenly occurred to me that my pet detective work was no longer an idea, an experiment, or even an important cause. The deep love for animals that God wove into my DNA was something He wanted to use to bless and comfort other people. From that moment forward I realized my pet detective work was no longer just a business or a cool career; it was my life purpose.

Chapter Ten
PET DETECTIVE IN THE PAPERS

When I was on patrol as a police officer, I felt cool, composed, and powerful. The high-energy, anything-can-happen nature of police work adrenalized me, even when the tasks were routine. I loved the fast-paced atmosphere and the times when I sped from emergency to emergency on the night shift, feeling like the world was on my shoulders. I thrived on the symphony of sirens, squealing tires, and the high-pitched voices that filled the police radio during a car chase. It felt good to give traffic tickets to reckless drivers who deserved them, and I felt immense satisfaction—okay, perhaps just a latent dose of revenge—when I issued a $175 citation to a rude driver who had just called me an offensive name. It was good to be a cop.

But it was an entirely different thing to be a pet detective. Instead of pursuing people who wanted nothing to do with my "services" (everyone from drivers exceeding the speed limit to burglars and participants in barroom brawls), I was responding to pet owners who needed and actually appreciated my help. When I gave a traffic ticket, I was likely to get a curse in response. When I tracked a lost pet, I was met with genuine gratitude. When I made an arrest, I was often despised. When I found a lost pet, I was highly praised. As a cop, I felt a little like Dirty Harriet. But when I responded to pet detective cases, I felt like Mother Theresa with a bloodhound.

Almost every missing-pet investigation I worked brought more encouragement from pet owners. Some were elated to have found their beloved pets alive and well, and others were grieving the confirmation of their worst fears, but regardless, they were all grateful for my help. I even began to entertain the idea of making my new hobby a full-time job. I was sure there was a need for the kind of service I could offer, and equally certain that no one else was providing it.

It made sense to me that an animal shelter would be my best base of operations. The first place a pet owner looks when a pet goes missing is the local humane society. Even though the shelter closest to me hadn't let me put up my flyers, I figured looking for a position on-staff would be a completely different concept, and one that might be better received. I had a lot to learn, I guess, about the minimal funding most shelters have and the legions of dedicated volunteers who keep most of them operational. So I approached a local humane society and asked if they would hire me as a pet detective. The director was kind enough not to laugh, but immediately dismissed my bizarre suggestion.

When I mentioned my offer—and its rejection—to a friend, she did laugh. "Most shelters can barely afford the food and veterinary bills for the animals in their care," she said. "I've volunteered at the SPCA for years, and I promise you there is no money in any animal shelter budget to pay a salary for a job like that."

Her assessment was fair enough, but she took it one step further. "You're having a pipe dream," she chuckled, "if you think you can make a living as a pet detective."

I hung up the phone, and after a minute or so of self-pity, started making notes on how to start a nonprofit organization of my own. No one was going to tell me what I could or couldn't do! It became my mission to prove my friend wrong, mostly because she was so darned smug that I couldn't do it.

"You want to see a pipe dream?" I asked out loud. Rachel raised her head from a warm, snuggly nap on the couch. "Watch this!" Instead of developing a local business as a pet detective where I could only help pet owners in a small area, I resolved to pioneer the nation's first national nonprofit organization dedicated to lost pet recovery.

Within three months, I had dissolved my Pet Pursuit business, recruited a board of directors, and founded the National Center for Missing Pets (NCMP). During the early stages of our development, I contacted local television stations and newspapers in the hope of generating media attention. In addition to finding volunteers, I wanted pet owners to know that my services existed. In November 1997, I contacted Andreas Tzortzis, a reporter at the *San Francisco Chronicle*, to ask if he would run a story on my pet detective work. Andreas was very interested in my story. He asked if he could come along and watch Rachel and me work a search, and of course, I agreed.

But first I needed a lost pet to search for. I picked up a copy of the *San Jose Mercury News* and scanned the "lost cat" classified ads. I reached a couple of voice mails but couldn't bring myself to leave a message. I figured if I left a message saying I was a pet detective, people would assume it was a prank. On the third call, a woman answered the phone.

"Hello, ma'am," I said with as much professionalism as I could muster. "My name is Kat Albrecht. I'm a police officer with eight years of experience in training dogs to look for missing people. I recently trained one of my dogs to track missing pets."

The woman was silent. I wondered if she thought I was a nut.

"I saw your ad in the paper about your lost cat," I continued, "and my dog Rachel has already located several missing cats. I normally charge a fee to conduct a search for a missing pet. But I've got a newspaper reporter from the *Chronicle* who wants to come along and watch my dog work. I'm willing to come out and search for your cat for free."

The woman was still silent. I began to feel foolish; my confidence waned.

"I know this all sounds really unusual," I said apologetically, not sure what to make of her continued silence. "We really don't need to do this if you're not comfortable."

"No, no," the woman said, her voice sounding choked with emotion. "That's not it. This has been a really rough month. My nineteen-year-old son died three weeks ago. His cat, Gizmo, disappeared the day before he died. Gizmo is the only part of my son that I have left. I really need to find this cat."

I was stunned. Anyone who pays for a lost-cat ad could be expected to take the loss seriously, but I couldn't have anticipated the gravity of the situation. The woman, Janet Leverich, gave me directions to her home in Saratoga.

I made arrangements with Andreas to meet me at Janet's house the following morning. It was raining steadily as I drove from Santa Cruz to Saratoga, a suburb of San Jose located thirty minutes from my home. Andreas arrived within a few minutes, and after a brief greeting we knocked on the front door.

Janet invited us in. She and her husband, Lyle, showed us pictures of their son Doug and Gizmo, a gray tabby cat. They avoided talking about the death of their son and focused on the disappearance of Gizmo. The grief of both losses was evident in their voices and in their eyes.

"This cat means so much to us," Janet told me. "My son loved Gizmo. We wonder if Gizmo might even have left because he sensed my son was so ill."

A cat that looked like Gizmo had been spotted at a park a half mile down the road. Janet had been told that a family with a small child had picked up the friendly cat and had taken it home with them. The cat was a gray tabby, just like Gizmo.

"Maybe your dog will take us to the park," Janet said. I could hear the hope in her voice—hope that Rachel would help us determine that Gizmo was the cat from the park, hope that Gizmo was alive and well and self-adopted by a loving family.

"Maybe," I said. "We'll give Rachel Gizmo's scent and see where she leads us." I didn't want to be too optimistic. It seemed to me that a half mile was just too far for most cats to wander on their own. Andreas, the reporter, watched and listened in silence as I conducted my investigation. I determined where Gizmo spent most of his time and the exact area that was his established territory. I learned that Gizmo slept on a pile of drapes and I used that as my scent article. Gizmo had been missing for three weeks, and although his scent trail would be too weak to work, I could still use Rachel in an area-search mode to check the high-probability areas within Gizmo's territory.

The rain peppered my jacket as I harnessed Rachel, presented Gizmo's scent under her nose, and gave the search command. In spite of her dislike for the rain, Rachel worked with eagerness. For over an hour we scoured the area. We checked the front and back yards in the neighborhood and a vacant field behind Gizmo's home. We searched just about everywhere, except the house next door. Those particular neighbors had not been home for Janet to obtain permission for us to enter their property.

"Maybe we could go by and knock on the door. They might be home by now," I suggested. It was the last area to search. Janet and Lyle knocked on the door while Andreas and I waited with Rachel on the front lawn. The neighbor came to the door and said it was fine for us to check her yard. I gave Rachel the search command and we started to work past a group of heavy shrubs in the front yard. Suddenly, Rachel turned her head as she picked up an airborne scent. She pulled me toward the edge of a large bush. There, partially concealed, was the body of a gray tabby cat. The cat was wearing a blue collar.

"Oh no," I said as I came to an abrupt stop. No one else had seen the cat yet, including Janet, who was right behind me. "Was Gizmo wearing a blue collar?"

"Yes, why?" Janet said with urgency, rushing up to see what I had found. The cat was Gizmo.

Janet let out an agonized wail, the kind of cry I had heard before, at accident and crime scenes, when a family member first learned that a loved one had died. She collapsed against her husband. Andreas stood back and watched in silence.

"Can you tell how long he's been dead?" Janet finally asked me.

"No," I replied. "I'm sorry, but I really can't." The cold, damp winter conditions had preserved Gizmo's body, but my hunch was that he had probably been dead since the day he failed to come home.

Lyle helped Janet to her feet and began walking her back toward their house.

A few moments later, he returned to the lawn alone.

"I am so very sorry," I told Lyle. "Please tell Janet I will be praying for her."

"I will," he answered. "Thank you for your help."

In most cases when we found a deceased pet, the owner was thankful for the closure. Gizmo was the first case where finding the body only seemed to magnify the family's pain. I wished I could have left Janet and Lyle with their belief that Gizmo was still alive. For the first time, I wished a search had been a bust. It would have been better not to have found the missing cat at all. I was filled with remorse, guilt-ridden for adding to the couple's grief.

Andreas offered to buy me lunch at a nearby restaurant so that he could complete his interview with me. We walked into the restaurant in silence. I sat down wearily in the booth. Andreas just looked at me. After gathering my thoughts and controlling my emotions, I broke the silence.

"I'm sure you were planning to write a cute, Ace Ventura-type story for the paper," I said. "But you can see that there's a very serious side to this work. The people I help deeply love their pets. Their grief is not very different from the grief of losing a family member. People who don't love animals may find this hard to understand."

"To be honest," Andreas told me. "My assignment *was* to write a lighthearted article. But I don't think I can do that now. I'll talk to my editor and see what I can do."

Andreas kept his promise. Three days later, I opened the *Chronicle* and read an article titled "Cop Tracks Missing Pets in Off Time." It was fair, truthful, and it didn't gloss over the sometimes somber realities of my pet searches. I was deeply grateful to the reporter for taking me seriously and for not treating my efforts like a joke. It felt good to be respected.

Chapter Eleven
A CHANGE IN DIRECTION

Thankfully, the serious nature of my pet detective work was sometimes offset by charming and bizarre events, a fact that served to save my sanity and arm me with ammunition for interviews. In one case, a woman who found an unwelcome "package" of dog poop on her property called and asked me to bring a search dog out to backtrack the scent trail to determine whose rude dog had left a deposit on her lawn. In another case, a documentary producer asked if I would fly with my dogs to Florida to track "Skunk Ape," the Everglades version of Bigfoot. We did not respond on either of these cases.

But we did respond to search for Bret, a bearded dragon on the lam who had jumped from his owner's arms and disappeared in heavy brush. Bret's owner was a former Hollywood actor who dressed his lizard in doll clothing because Bret was a "star." Bret had once appeared in an MTV music video. I know this for a fact because Rachel and I had to sit and watch his video before we could start our search.

And then there was Barry. In this case, I was called and asked to work an undercover pet detective operation. Every cop loves to go under cover. The thrill of police work combined with the danger of being exposed means double the excitement. Throw in a deadly snake, and an adrenaline junky like me is having the time of her life.

Barry was a *very* large boa constrictor who slithered to freedom from his glass enclosure at a California zoo. The entire staff of the place spent three weeks frantically looking for their missing snake—with the zoo still open to the public—before they called to see if I could help them. To this day, I'm still sworn to secrecy about the name and location of the facility.

One of the zoo supervisors heard about my pet detective work and called to see if Rachel could search for a snake. She made it very clear that this was sensitive information and that they did not want the media or the public to be aware that they had a boa constrictor loose in their zoo. Once I explained what I would need and what they could expect of Rachel, we made arrangements that I would show up the following morning. The supervisor told me to enter a particular gate and look for the security guard kiosk. I was to park there and ask the security guard to page Darla Robbins, who would come and meet me at the gate. And there was one more thing...the supervisor asked if I could respond as discreetly as possible. I agreed.

I left my orange pet detective vest at home. I took Rachel's harness but left her orange "Search Dog" shabrack behind. I skipped the magnetic "PET DETECTIVES" business signs that I normally slapped on the doors of my truck as I headed out to search for a lost pet. I didn't even take my yellow backpack that had a tiny little blue "Search Dog" patch on it. Instead, I stuffed all my search gear into a plain khaki canvas bag, loaded my pet Weimaraner into my civilian truck, and hit the highway, ready to spend a day at the zoo.

There was only one problem. My personalized license plate read "PET HNTR" and my bumper was draped with a reflective SEARCH & RESCUE sticker from my old search-and-rescue days. I wasn't about to scrape off a sticker for one search, nor was I willing to cover my license plates. After traveling a few hours, I finally pulled into the designated gate and spotted the kiosk with a Security placard above the door. I walked up to the security officer.

To the left of the kiosk, standing only fifteen yards away, was a group of about thirty young adults. I suspected they were waiting for the rest of their group since none of them were purchasing tickets and entering the zoo. But I was very aware of their presence and wanted to make sure I did not indicate to the security guard just why I was there. Undercover means undercover—I wasn't even going to let security know what I was there for.

"Search and Rescue?" he asked. I wasn't sure if he had a reading problem or if he simply wanted me to explain why the words were on my bumper.

"Yes," was all I said. I didn't want him to know that I had a dog in the back of my truck until after I had met with the zoo employee. She could explain to him later what the nature of my visit was about if policy would permit.

"I'm here to see Darla Robbins," I said as I showed him my driver's license. The guard smiled, wrote down my name, and told me he would page

Darla for me. I turned and had walked only five steps toward my truck when I heard a blaring voice come across the public address system, reverberating through the entire zoo:

"Darla Robbins, please come to gate three. The lady with the dog trained to find lost snakes is here."

I froze in my tracks. My cover was blown. I just knew that someone in the crowd of people standing by the kiosk was already calling the local news station. Before I even had a chance to unload my dog from my truck, I'd exposed the zoo's secret!

As it turned out, the zoo was closed that day to the public. The crowd standing by the security kiosk was a group of zoo employees and a few volunteer docents. They were all already aware that Barry was missing and completely unfazed by the PA announcement about my intentions. Moments later, Darla, a petite blond woman in her mid-twenties, met me at the gate. After a short briefing, I grabbed my canvas bag, unloaded Rachel, and followed Darla into the zoo.

The zoo was a jungle of ferns, flowers, trees and thick brush. Misters kept the area cool and finches and pigeons pecked at discarded popcorn crumbs on the ground. A small flock of peacocks strutted around, and a male squawked in protest with a loud screeching noise when he saw Rachel. Darla gave me a mini-tour as we passed by cages that housed wildcats, wolves, antelope, and other animals.

The snake hut was a small building about the size of an average living room. Visitors could view the snakes in their giant aquariums from a cool, covered patio. Barry had somehow pushed aside the screen from his glass cage. It was believed that he could have escaped into the ceiling or walls and that he might well still be inside the hut somewhere. Because of this, I had requested that all the snakes be removed from the building so that I could use Rachel in a detection mode. I knew that one of Barry's snakeskins was available, and I would use that as my scent article.

Darla took me through the locked door of the hut and we entered the area where the caretakers would normally access the snakes to feed them and clean their cages. I glanced down and saw that Rachel's nose was already quivering. I also noticed several tennis-ball-sized holes in the wall.

"Last week we brought a vet who had a scope-like camera," Darla said. "We drilled holes all over the place to look inside the walls and in the ceiling, but we couldn't see Barry."

"Where is Barry's snakeskin?" I asked. "I want to let Rachel sniff it so she knows what she is searching for."

Darla opened the bottom drawer of a metal desk and took out a paper sack. She reached inside and pulled out a snakeskin that, I swear, at its widest part was the size of one of my thighs. I suddenly understood just *why* the staff of the zoo didn't want the media or the paying public to know that Barry the boa was missing. There would be no "Reward: Lost Snake" posters on this case.

After harnessing Rachel, I presented her with the mammoth snakeskin. I suspected that trying to give her a scent article would be a lost cause. The room probably still smelled like one gigantic snake and expecting a detection dog to pinpoint the scent of a stationary snake in the midst of other odors was asking a bit much.

Rachel snuffled the dry skin intently and began casting around the room. At one point, she lifted her nose high and, to my surprise, she planted her front paws on the top of the desk as she jutted her nose high towards the ceiling and rapidly sniffed. Darla climbed up and, using a flashlight, peered through a few of the holes that had been drilled in the ceiling, but there was no sign of Barry. I took Rachel back to the place she had alerted but she did not alert again. It was likely that she was picking up leftover scent from the other snakes that had been taken out of the room. After allowing her to sniff around on her own, I began to direct Rachel to sniff in the many holes in the sides of the wall.

"Check this," I commanded as I pointed to a hole. Rachel would stand on her hind legs in order to poke her nose in the hole and give it a whiff. We did this through the room, checking all the holes, but didn't come up with any alerts. There was a small hole in the floor that Darla suspected Barry had used to slither out of the hut and into the free world. Based on Rachel's work, this seemed quite possible.

Darla asked if we could start to check around the premises to see if Rachel showed any interest. I agreed, knowing that this would be a much easier and realistic detection problem for my dog. We walked out the door and Rachel immediately pulled me over to one of the giant wooden snake boxes. She sniffed through the wire mesh top, wiggling her tail with excitement, as I watched a big snake move below her nose. I told Rachel she was a good girl but she had found the wrong animal, and walked her to an area away from the maze of displaced snakes. A few employees had been watching our search work and as soon as we were finished in the hut, Darla put them back to work in putting all the snakes back where they belonged.

For the next two hours, we searched the zoo and found no trace of any snakes outside of the vicinity of the snake hut. Darla was grateful that we had tried and seemed comforted to know that Barry probably wasn't lingering under any of the zoo's rides or exhibits, waiting to surprise an unsuspecting visitor.

Usually requests to utilize my search dogs, from law enforcement agencies and from pet owners, floated in weeks, sometimes months, apart. But there was one day at the office when my two jobs collided.

I had just worked a ten-hour graveyard shift patrolling the university, and I was exhausted. As I fed my dogs their breakfast, I noticed that during the night someone had left a message on my answering machine. A woman who had lost her toy poodle wanted me to come out and search for her lost dog ASAP.

I crawled into bed thinking that after I'd had a couple hours of sleep, I'd call her back and search that afternoon.

About an hour later, my pager went off.

"Santa Cruz PD has a man armed with a gun who ran into the woods," the dispatcher told me. "They want you to respond with your bloodhound."

As I slipped on my clothes, I couldn't help but smile at my dilemma. Should I search for the poodle first, or the man with the gun?

"Man with a gun...toy poodle...man with a gun...toy poodle," I asked A.J. and Rachel, who were both curled in a nest on the edge of my bed. "What do *you* want to do first?"

Most people would agree that the man with a gun case was more urgent than the search for a lost dog, but try telling *that* to someone who just lost their toy poodle! I searched for the man with the gun first, and the poodle a few hours later. But as I crawled into bed for the second time that day—knowing I would have to be at work in less than three hours—I realized I would probably need to decide pretty soon what I wanted to be when I grew up. As it turned out, I never did have to decide. Fate stepped in and rather violently shoved me in the direction I was to take.

On December 30, 1997, I reported to work at the university for my usual graveyard shift. As always, I changed into my uniform fifteen minutes before I was scheduled to go on duty. I put on my leather duty belt, checked my pistol to make sure it was loaded, snapped it into its holster, and headed downstairs to the briefing room.

I said hello to the sergeant on duty and settled in, expecting few or no calls for the evening. Because it was Christmas break, the students and most of the faculty were not on campus. This was typically the slowest week of the year.

About an hour into my shift a call came over my radio.

"Be on the lookout for a possible DUI," said the on-duty dispatcher. "Reporting party states a very intoxicated female is attempting to leave the faculty housing apartments in a red vehicle."

The faculty housing apartments were just down the street from the police station. I jogged out the door, hopped into my patrol car, and headed that way.

The dispatcher's voice came over my radio again. "RP states that the female just left in a red Ford hatchback, unknown license number."

The drunk driver was headed my way. I stopped, turned off my headlights, and waited in the dark at the edge of the parking lot. From my position, I had a clear view of any cars leaving the faculty housing apartments. Within thirty seconds, a pair of headlights appeared as the car turned onto the main road, heading in my direction.

It was a red Ford hatchback. I turned on my headlights as the car passed directly in front of me. The speed limit was twenty-five but this car was clearly doing at least forty-five. I pulled out and accelerated to catch up with her.

The hatchback drifted off the right shoulder of the road, overcorrected and swerved over the double solid lines into the oncoming lane. I hadn't even turned on my emergency lights yet because I was not close enough to see the license plate. But now that the car was recklessly out of control, I activated my emergency lights.

The driver overcorrected to avoid oncoming traffic. She jerked her steering wheel hard to the right and slammed on the brakes. The hatchback skidded, careened off the roadway, and broke through a barbed-wire fence. It slid between two stone pillars and crashed into an antique wooden wagon under a historic building. It had been a very short, very dangerous drive for the intoxicated woman behind the wheel.

I pulled up behind the car and shone my spotlight in the driver's rear-view mirror, illuminating a single female occupant. To my surprise, as I approached the car, the backup lights came on. Apparently she intended to keep driving.

"Stop the car!" I yelled at the woman. She continued to try to back up, but the car was stuck. I thumped her window with my flashlight. She stopped accelerating and jerked her head around to face me. Apparently she hadn't been aware that I was there. I opened the car door.

"Stop the car," I repeated. She just looked at me with a blank stare, so I reached in and turned the key myself, cutting off the engine.

"Awww craaaap," the woman drawled. It had taken a few moments for her brain to register that I was a police officer.

"Are you all right?" I asked her. She didn't appear to be hurt, but I knew she had taken a pretty good slam.

"I'm okay," she said, her voice thick with alcohol.

I took her elbow and guided her out of the car. "Are you sure you aren't hurt? I can have an ambulance crew come take a look at you if you need it."

"No, I'm all right," the woman said as she struggled to find solid footing. To test her level of awareness, I asked her what had happened. She said she didn't remember, then told me that she was an English professor from another campus. I administered the routine field sobriety tests, which included the heel-to-toe walk, reciting the alphabet, the fingertip-to-nose, and other balance and dexterity tests. She failed all of them.

"I have one more test for you," I lied. "Turn around and put both of your arms behind your back, interlacing your fingers." The woman complied. I removed my handcuffs from their case, snapped them on both of her wrists and told her she was under arrest for driving under the influence.

"Come on, officer!" the suspect half begged, half demanded. "You can just drive me home. You don't need to arrest me."

"Sorry," I said. "Watch your head." I guided her into the back seat of my patrol car. When she saw that I was serious about taking her to jail, all attempts at politeness and cooperation were over. Instead, the English professor in my backseat showed her higher education language skills and swore like a sailor, alternately threatening and berating me for taking her into custody. She refused to answer my routine booking questions such as her phone number, social security number, and address. She kept asking for a cigarette and said she was thirsty and wanted some water.

"My head hurts," she complained. "Did you guys hit me on the head?" At that point I became concerned. She had collided with the wagon at about thirty miles per hour. She had refused medical treatment, but I knew that her agitated behavior, although likely due to the alcohol, might be a sign of a head injury. I also knew that thirst is a sign of hypovolemic shock due to internal bleeding. Rather than take any chances with her health, I immediately drove her straight to the hospital.

"I want a cigarette," the suspect announced as I guided her out of my patrol car and toward the emergency room door.

"You'll have to wait until you get to jail." I wasn't about to tell her smoking was not allowed at the jail and that she was in for a nicotine withdrawal nightmare.

She stopped in her tracks.

"I want my cigarettes NOW," she demanded, like a two-year-old about to throw a tantrum. I had to use a pain compliance "control hold" just to get her inside. Control holds are used by police officers to overcome physical resistance in a violent suspect by bending a wrist, an arm, or fingers in order to move or arrest a suspect. They inflict pain but no damage. The squeezing of the professor's fingers was uncomfortable for her, but it enabled me to move her inside the hospital. She was screaming as we entered the emergency room. All the nurses, doctors, patients, and a sheriff's deputy simultaneously turned to look at the noisy disruption that had just walked through the door.

The woman was swearing at the top of her lungs, punctuating her comments with high-pitched screams, and getting more out of control by the minute.

"DUI involved in car accident," was all I had to say to the nurse behind the desk. She quickly escorted us to an empty room.

The suspect screeched and lurched for the door.

Another officer appeared and offered to assist me. He took the suspect's other arm and helped pull her back to the gurney.

Furious, she began to kick at both of us. Two other security guards rushed in to help, but before they could grab my suspect's legs, she took another kick at me.

To avoid the blow, I twisted and jerked away. As I did, I felt my lower back go out. Instantly, I felt a burning pain through my back and down the backs of my legs, something I had never felt before.

By the time a doctor examined the drunk driver, an hour later, I knew I was going to need medical attention, too. The pain in my back was excruciating, but I was determined to see my case through. Two security guards helped me get the woman back into my patrol car and I headed to the county jail. I radioed ahead, knowing I would need help when we arrived.

Four correctional deputies met us in the enclosed area where police cars unload prisoners who are being escorted into jail. When the deputies approached, the suspect was on her back, her hands still cuffed behind her, using both feet to try to kick out the back window of my patrol car.

The deputies pulled her from the car and maneuvered her into the jail.

I went to the doctor the next day and was immediately put on light duty. I was instructed to come to work in plain clothes, perform light office work, and take police reports over the phone until my back was better. But over the next few weeks, the pain in my back persisted. I developed numbness in my foot and pains that radiated from my lower back down to my left foot.

All the training and all searches with my dogs came to a grinding halt. My back needed time to heal. But as the weeks turned into months, it didn't seem to be getting any better. Instead of working practice trails and searches with Rachel, A.J. and Chase, we all huddled together in my living room, watching television and fattening up.

My dogs, to their credit, never complained for a minute. Some dogs' behavior is directly tied to the amount of exercise they get, giving credence to the theory that a tired dog is a good dog. But mine were wonderful. They seemed to understand that I wasn't able to take them for the long walks, jogs, and training exercises they were used to. Rachel and Chase snuggled at my feet on the couch, sisters to the core. A.J. slobbered solemnly on a dog bed beside me, always keeping an eye in my direction, as if a missing person might crop up at any moment and jar us both back into our old, more exciting routine.

The other officers on campus often asked me when I would be returning to patrol, but I had no answer. I felt helpless, frustrated, and even guilty that my inability to work forced others to work overtime. At one point, about four months after my injury, I actually lied to the doctor and told him that I was "pain free." I wanted to return to patrol and to working my dogs badly enough that I was willing to endure whatever discomfort came with the job.

"Good," the doctor said. "But I'm going to give you a physical performance test." For liability reasons, he couldn't let me go back to work just because I said I was pain free. I would have to prove it.

The test involved walking, running, climbing, and lifting for starters. It was an eight-hour test, but I only made it to the fifth hour. I couldn't perform many of the required movements. Climbing caused severe back pain, and running caused a sharp pain to shoot from my lower back to my left foot. I flunked the performance test. Five months after my injury, the insurance company finally agreed to pay for an MRI of my back. The MRI revealed that I had herniated a disc. I was put into physical therapy with the hope that I could rehabilitate my back.

Because of my injury, I had to turn down many requests to search for missing pets. At the next NCMP meeting, the board members and I began to devise a new plan of action. I would train a group of volunteer pet detectives who could work Rachel for me. Because Rachel was fully trained, it would be simple for me to train someone else to read her body language. I would go along on the searches to observe and coach from a safe distance.

In October 1998, nine months after the night I had hurt my back trying to restrain the drunk driver, I received the news that I had feared. The doctor determined that the damage to the disc in my back was permanent. All attempts at rehabilitation had failed to get me to a point where I was pain free.

The doctor recommended a medical retirement. I was devastated. Training and working bloodhounds to track criminals was my number one passion. Even though I loved my pet detective adventures, I had worked myself to the bone to make it as a cop, and largely defined myself by that accomplishment.

On December 30, 1998, I spent my final day as a sworn police officer. The police department staff gave me a nice going-away party where they presented me with a gift—they had a trophy shop suspend my duty badge in a block of clear acrylic. What once was a symbol of power and authority was now a paperweight. Although I appreciated the gift, I went home to my cabin, sat down with my dogs, and cried.

I hated to give up the career I had worked so hard for, and I was terrified to lose the security of a full-time job with benefits. Most of all, it was hard for me to swallow the fact that a simple twist of my back had ended my career. I thought it would have been a little easier to cope if I had sustained some type of heroic injury while saving a person's life instead of being the victim of a combative drunk driver.

When I was able to accept that my time as a police officer was over, I knew what I was going to do next. It was time to throw myself heart and soul into my life as a full-time, bona fide, pipe dreaming pet detective!

Chapter Twelve
FULL INVESTIGATION

It's hard to get too excited about anything when your body hurts and your medication makes your brain fuzzy and having lost your job makes you crabby. There were months after I was forcibly retired from the police force when I was pretty wrapped up in my own misery. But the highlight of that time was when first one volunteer, and then several more, came into my life, all wanting to be trained to search for lost pets.

The first student I took on was Becky Hiatt, the office manager for my veterinarian, Charlie Miller, at the Scotts Valley Vet Clinic. I knew Becky, but just on a professional level from the all too many occasions when I took my critters to the vet. While waiting for Dr. Miller, I would share pet detective stories with Becky, who seemed intrigued. On one such occasion, after blabbering and bragging about Rachel, I ended my war story by asking Becky, "So, would you like to come along on a search sometime?"

Becky was an eager student. Without her having much training, we responded to search for a cat named Buster who had escaped from his home in Aptos. With a trace of melancholy, I handed the leash over to Becky and shouted occasional instructions from the flat ground below as Becky guided Rachel to search the steep, brush and rock-filled terrain that extended high above the client's house.

Becky and Rachel found Buster, alive and well, though very panicked at the sight of his four-legged rescuer. Rachel flushed him out from where he had been crouched and hidden in a section of tall weeds. I was torn—a little jealous that I was not handling Rachel when she made the find, yet excited to know that our search work could be accomplished with someone else working my dog.

Not long after I started working with Becky, A.J. and I were asked to make an appearance at a doggy adoption event in Half Moon Bay, a small coastal town located an hour north of Santa Cruz. At that event, I met four women who all said they wanted to train their own dogs to locate lost pets. I was surprised to find so many eager students, but very willing to do everything I could to teach them what I knew. After that initial meeting, every Thursday morning I drove north along the westernmost edge of the continental United States, up the magnificent coastal Highway 1, to meet with these rookies. This was going to be a new venture for me, to take someone else's dog and teach it to trail the scent of a pet—especially since these dogs had not already been trained to trail people.

We worked through the foggy and chilly winter months, tromping through a large county park, sometimes even trailing a scent along the beaches of the Pacific Ocean. But most of the time we worked in the massive park, through fields of brown weeds bordered by Douglas firs, redwoods, oak trees, and California buckeyes. When spring eventually rolled around, the dull, weedy fields were transformed into acres of wildflowers that included wood roses, sun cups, and California poppies. I relished my trips to Half Moon Bay, both to see how much my volunteers and their search dogs had learned as well as how many new wildflowers had bloomed.

The dogs taught me as much as I taught them. Leo, a German shepherd mix, quickly made it clear that he was interested in dog scent of a different kind. With feigned excitement, Leo would snuffle the scent article at the start of a scent trail, take off like a rocket, run about twenty yards, slow down to a walk, and proceed to leisurely sniff around until he found the precise spot where another dog had peed. Just when I was ready to give up on him, Leo's owner, Sheryl Carver, mentioned that Leo loved cats.

So I took my cat Yogi to one of the training sessions. When Leo found Yogi, his whole back end wagged in giant propeller-like circles. No amount of dog-pee scent could distract Leo from searching for a cat. Leo taught me that some dogs would excel at trailing dog scent and some would excel at detecting cats, but very few dogs possessed Rachel's talent for doing both. Leo was the first of many "cat-detection" dogs that I went on to train.

Kelsey, a golden retriever, loved to play with other pups. She went into a frenzy whenever someone ran away and hid around a corner with a dog. In training her, I discovered that the best candidates for trailing dogs were the dog-park-types who lived to play. I developed a new system of evaluating search dogs for trailing work. I would instruct someone to run away with another dog as I watched the potential search dog I was evaluating. I would only pass the potential search dog if it struggled and jumped and became so excited that it would try to get away in order to chase after the other dog.

I also learned that when training dogs to trail the scent of another dog, I could use similar methods to those I had used to train dogs to trail the scent of a person. However, instead of a hunk of cheese at the end of the trail, these search dogs were rewarded with what they considered the ultimate reward—playtime with the "lost" dog they had found. Kelsey excelled in training and ultimately went on to successfully trail several missing dogs in Northern California, earning a great reputation. These early experiences of training other handler's dogs to find lost pets ultimately paved the way for the publication of my book, *Dog Detectives: Train Your Dog to Find Lost Pets.*

In addition to the Half Moon Bay volunteers and a handful of Santa Cruz volunteers, I had two new key players. When I left the police force, I had to make a decision about A.J. and Chase. My first award-winning, dedicated bloodhound and his dedicated protégée deserved better than to spend the rest of their lives sniffing the flowers in my backyard. I could have donated one or both to another bloodhound handler who could actively work them on criminal and missing person cases, or I could have sold them to a police agency looking for trained bloodhounds.

But there was no way I was going to give up my dogs after all we'd been through together. It had taken me years to figure out the complexities of A.J.'s aloof personality, but by the time I hurt my back, I could read him like a book and I loved him like a child. And Chase was so committed to me, and I to her, I could never give her up.

And so, by default, A.J. and Chase became pet detectives, too. They needed a job to do, and I needed more dogs to search for lost pets. To their credit, neither hound ever hesitated at the change of direction. Chase, who had always been "dog aggressive," which is quite rare for a bloodhound, was so excited about following the scent of another dog that she reminded me of Winnie the Pooh's Tigger. When she saw a stray dog walk by our backyard, Chase became so agitated that she would bounce straight up and down with pogo stick-like legs. When given the scent of another dog, Chase dragged me along the scent trail with equal enthusiasm.

A.J.'s response was slightly different. He was such a seasoned pro that nothing seemed to faze him. All I had to do was give him a pet's scent and say "Search!" and A.J. would follow the scent as if it were just another human. His demeanor was all Eeyore, a sluggish determination that translated to, "Of course, I'll find whatever you want."

A.J.'s very first pet search was a sad success. A diabetic indoor-only cat named Marmalade had escaped out the back door of his home in Los Gatos. His owner, Kennon, was distraught. Unable to eat, sleep, or work, Kennon begged me to help her find her favorite cat. Because of my injury, I was unable to work A.J. myself. So the next day, when Becky was off work, we arrived at Kennon's house with A.J.

"That dog will never find that cat," were the first words I heard when I stepped out of my truck. It was a skeptical relative of Kennon who apparently did not believe in the scenting ability of my dog. That comment didn't exactly boost my confidence. This search took place before I'd had the chance to put A.J. through any lost-pet training. To be honest, I wasn't even sure myself whether A.J. would understand that I wanted him to follow cat scent instead of human scent. For the entire seven years of his life, I'd always had him find people. Now, just like Kea had been asked to suddenly follow A.J.'s scent, I was about to ask A.J. to follow the scent of a cat.

To make things more difficult, Becky had never handled A.J. before. I did my best to coach her by shouting instructions to her as my faithful bloodhound led her and Kennon from the point of escape, through the backyard, under a fence, down a steep ravine, under a barbed-wire fence, and then north into a brushy area where they disappeared.

Moments later, I heard wailing. A.J. had led Becky and Kennon right up to Marmalade's body. It was difficult to witness such a sad ending, but Kennon made a point of profusely thanking us for helping her recover Marmalade's body. "Now," she said through her tears, "I can bury my cat and sleep again."

In showing other people like Becky how to handle my search dogs, I realized just how unconventional our training had been. First, volunteers had to learn about Rachel's multipurpose nose. Given the correct commands,

Rachel was capable of searching in several different ways. She could conduct an area search for decomposition and pinpoint it with the alerts she had used in her cadaver searches. By simply saying, "Find the kitty," Rachel would focus on scouring an area for any hidden cats. She could just as easily conduct an area search for any specific smell I presented to her—be it a lost cat, iguana, or ferret. Her scent discrimination skills were near perfect, and since we had started searching primarily for lost pets, a job that Rachel loved, I knew I could trust her to stick to the scent she was assigned. Lastly, Rachel could follow a scent trail. She was far too dainty to be a bloodhound, and her nose was 100% Weimaraner, but she could trail nearly as well as A.J. with the right command.

It was actually the dedication of the volunteers to my lost-pet cause that kept me productive. As my body slowly began to give me more latitude in what I was able to do, their companionship and enthusiasm drove me to get out and push myself to work with my dogs again.

As I became even more immersed in pet detective work, it became clear that using a search dog to find lost pets was just the tip of the iceberg. Many pet owners believed that a bloodhound was *the* answer to locating their lost pet but, as is the case in lost-person searches, the search dogs were only one tool in an entire system used to find the missing. With this in mind, I began to experiment with additional law enforcement tactics and techniques. In every missing-pet investigation, I looked for and began to find physical evidence. Some hair fibers caught in the jagged edges of an old wooden fence indicated the precise point where a dog escaped from his yard. Cobwebs in the opening of a pipe ruled out the pipe as a potential search area for a missing cat.

While my police training had taught me how to look for physical evidence, my training in search-and-rescue management techniques also came in handy in lost-pet searches. Lost-person search techniques include the use of trackers, high-tech equipment, search dogs and the study of statistics, probabilities, and lost-person behavior. A search manager will determine which areas should be searched first based on the probable behavior of the missing person. This, of course, depends on the person—a hunter or hiker, a confused senior, and a frightened child will all behave differently when lost. Based on what we know about the person, we determine the "high probability areas" where these groups of missing people are most likely to be found.

The same kind of search probability theory could be applied to pet cases. In some cases, the logic was obvious, like when the mechanic from the auto shop told me point blank that he knew his dog Sky would never cross a railroad trestle. In other cases, lost-pet behavior was something I was still trying to sort out. Why did the injured cat dive under the neighbor's porch and stay there, while the injured husky took off and wandered for miles? And why did a Greyhound, a breed capable of running at speeds of thirty-five miles per hour, travel only four blocks when it was lost for two days? I wasn't sure, but I was determined to find out.

In my lost-pet searches, I also began to discover "high probability evidence"—signs that indicated a strong likelihood that a missing pet was in one particular location. I first noticed an example of this evidence in my own back yard a few years earlier. I had discovered a stick with a distinctive mustache-shaped arrangement of cat hair hanging from the underside. The stick was blocking a hole under my neighbor's deck, a favorite hiding place for Yogi. In order to get under the deck, Yogi had to rub against the stick every morning, day after day, as she passed under it. I discovered that this accumulation of cat hair fibers is physical evidence that can indicate a cat spends extensive time in a particular area. If Yogi ever disappeared, that deck would be one of the first places I would search.

I approached each lost-pet search trying to look for the same kind of information that had helped me locate missing persons. While the evidence and the anticipated behavior of pets are very different from those of people, I was learning more clearly with each case that the application of my search methods for lost humans was essentially the same for lost pets.

In homicide investigations, there's a combination of three seemingly unrelated behaviors that investigators call the homicidal triad. Identified by the FBI after interviews with more than three hundred and fifty serial killers, it says, in a nutshell, that if you have an adolescent white male who displays all three behaviors—cruelty to animals, fire setting, and bed-wetting beyond an appropriate age—that combination may be a precursor to homicidal tendencies. Thankfully, it doesn't always work that way. In his book *The Anatomy of Motive,* author and former FBI-agent John Douglas acknowledged that not every boy who displays the combination of these three behaviors will grow up to be a killer. But Douglas added, "The combination of the three was so prominent in our study subjects that we began recommending that a pattern of any two of them should raise a warning flag for parents and teachers."

It was theories like the homicidal triad and the dozens of others I had used in law enforcement that got me thinking about how I could assess the behavior of lost pets and somehow find a way to predict what they were going to do next. As with the FBI theory, there are few hard-and-fast rules in any investigation, but there are lots of theories that can make it easier to look at a case more objectively, and that helped me bring cases to resolution.

I started out by looking for a general formula that could be applied to any missing pet. I called it the "lost-pet-triad." In each missing-pet case, there were three interrelated behaviors that played a critical role in whether the pet was recovered: the actions of the pet, the actions of the owner/guardian, and the actions of the person who found or recovered that pet. By carefully examining the information I had about each factor, I was often able to predict what had likely happened to a lost dog or cat and what the chances were that the pet would be recovered. These interrelated behaviors are central to the on-line training courses that I currently use to train pet detectives, pet rescuers, private investigators, and other animal industry professionals.

When examining a case, first I'd look at the actions of the pet: Does it make a habit of escaping, or is it on its first foray into the world alone? Was it lost from its home, or from another location, like the veterinarian's office or a boarding facility? Was the pet injured? How did it run away: at breakneck speed due to panic from fireworks or at a slow crawl because it was exploring a scent? Was it a big, healthy dog, with the capability of traveling several miles a day, or an elderly, wounded cat, likely to get no further than twenty yards? Was it a show dog that might be stolen, or a mixed breed for which that was an unlikely factor? Was it a skittish dog that would run from strangers, or a wiggly-butt, friendly one? In each case, I weighed the pet's personality and the circumstances of the disappearance to try to predict which way it would go, how far, and how it would be received when someone found it.

Then came the actions of the pet owners. Did they put up flyers, contact the neighbors, canvass their entire property, or use social media to get the word out? Did they offer a reward of fifty dollars or five thousand dollars? Had they taken proactive measures and asked their veterinarian to microchip their pet, a simple procedure where an identification serial number is implanted under their pet's skin? And most important of all, did their pet wear a secure collar that included an identification tag with current owner information? Since a loose, stray dog almost always ends up in the hands of a human who finds it, there may be no better shot at getting a lost dog back than making sure the dog is easily identifiable with a collar and microchip before it gets lost.

There was also a very clear connection between the determination pet owners had to find their lost pet and their chances of succeeding. Persistence often paid off for those who would not give up.

In one case, a fourteen-year-old outdoor-access cat named Tony vanished from his home in Aptos. His owner, Catherine Murray, had already searched the neighborhood for Tony but was not able to find him. Three days later, after reading about my work in the paper, Catherine called and asked me to respond. I used Rachel in an area search and checked under decks, porches, and in heavy brush within a five-house radius of Tony's home. After conducting an extensive search of his territory, we determined that Tony was no longer there.

Catherine had mentioned that the day Tony vanished she had a roofer at her house doing repair work. The man had a van that he left open during his stay at the home, and Catherine suspected that Tony, who had a history of climbing on cars, might have climbed into the van. Catherine told me that she had already called the man and asked him to look in his van. The man had checked, but said Tony was not there. Because Rachel indicated that Tony was no longer in the area, it was obvious to me that the inside of the van was a high-probability search area.

I instructed Catherine to be aggressive and call the roofer again, suggesting that she simply ask him to tell her all the locations he had stopped at for the past three days. I figured that Tony could have jumped out of the van at one of the locations the roofer had stopped at. But Catherine took my suggestion to be aggressive even one step further. She drove over to the roofer's home. When she discovered the work van was parked out front but the man was not home, Catherine walked up to the van, peeked inside, and called Tony's name. Up popped the head of her very panicked, disoriented, and dehydrated elderly cat!

Catherine's behavior is a perfect example of how the actions of a pet owner, especially one who deeply loves his or her pet, will influence whether or not a lost pet will be found. Catherine recovered Tony because she was not afraid to a hire pet detective or to enter her neighbor's yards (with permission) to search for Tony herself, and she was willing to take matters into her own hands, without caring that the roofer would think she was a nutty cat lady.

But in many cases, I found that pet owners, upset, frustrated, inexperienced, and confused about how to go about a thorough search, seemed to throw all reasoning out the window and focus on theories that were unlikely, or, at best, just one of many possibilities. This was certainly the case with the intoxicated woman who stubbornly insisted that her blind Norwich terrier was tangled in the bushes by his leash, when all evidence pointed to the underground pipe system as the place where he could be found.

One of the most common tunnel-vision theories owners believe is that a pet has been stolen. Pet theft does happen. I know of clear cases of it, including dogs stolen from yards so they could be sold. Purebred dogs and show cats can be stolen to either breed or to resell for a profit (what is known as "pet flipping"). But while theft is a possibility in a few instances, my research has always indicated that in most missing pet cases, it is unlikely. I discovered that there is a pet theft myth that many people have bought into. Many have read or been told that pets are often stolen to be sold to research facilities for medical testing. Stories abound on the Internet about "Class B Dealers" stealing pets and selling them to research laboratories for profit. In reality, there are less than a dozen Class B Dealers in the entire USA, and those people typically breed their own dogs rather than steal pets to sell to laboratories. Pet theft is rare and is not a theory pet owners should pursue unless they have clear evidence.

In one case, a woman from Northern California called me in tears, saying her husband had lost their Labrador while hiking in the mountains. Before she spoke to me, she had called an animal organization where a staff member convinced her that her dog was likely already picked up by a Class B Dealer. It took me twenty minutes to calm this woman down and convince her that the odds that an animal dealer was hiking in the same area of the woods where her dog had just become lost were about as likely as the suggestion that the dog had been abducted by aliens. I was able to give her instructions on how and where to focus her search, advising her that there was a high likelihood her dog would be found by someone who assumed, because it was running alone in the wilderness, that it was unwanted and had been "dumped" there by an uncaring owner.

In that case and in countless others, the person who is most likely to hinder the return of a lost pet to its owner is often the well-meaning soul who finds it. The more cases I worked, the more research I conducted on what was being done to return lost pets to their owners. I was shocked to discover that many of the places where the owners of lost animals went for help were actually, unintentionally, exacerbating the lost-pet problem.

Animal shelters, for example, would hold a "stray" dog or cat for seventy-two hours, after which time they either adopted the animal out to a new family or destroyed it. If a pet owner was not able to get to the shelter within seventy-two hours, their chances of a happy reunion were slim to none. The national "Return to Owner" (RTO) rate for lost dogs reclaimed by their families at animal shelters is sixteen percent. For cats, the rate is much worse—just two percent of stray cats held at shelters have someone show up to reclaim them.

Rescue groups and individuals who pick up stray dogs and cats do a great job of saving animal lives, but many of them never transport found pets to the local animal shelter—the primary place where pet owners are searching. Oftentimes the person who picks up a stray dog wandering the streets assumes it was "abandoned" or they determine that because it was running loose, the owner must not want it too much or that they don't deserve to have the dog. These dogs seldom experience a happy reunion with their owner. Instead, a new family adopts them.

A perfect example of this was a case involving a golden retriever named Cash. One Labor Day weekend, Jan Gates, Cash's owner, took her dog to her cabin near Lake Tahoe, a forested area high in the Sierra Nevada Mountains. After letting Cash out of the cabin for an early morning potty break, and having taken his collar off due to an infection on his neck, Jan soon discovered that her dog was gone. Following an extensive, aggressive search for her dog, Jan learned that Cash was last seen bumming snacks at a gas station just off Interstate 80. She spent several days doing the usual routine—checking shelters, contacting vets, placing ads in newspapers from Lake Tahoe all the way west to Sacramento, a distance of about a hundred miles. Jan was even able to get airtime on a few radio stations, but as the days ticked away, the trail grew cold.

Finally, two weeks after Cash had disappeared, Jan received a lead. A woman working at a PETCO store said she remembered selling food to a couple who said they had found a male golden retriever on the freeway on Labor Day. Unfortunately, the couple paid with cash, so there was no way to trace them. Based on this lead, Jan developed an impressively aggressive strategy. Suspecting that the couple who had found the dog, which still wasn't confirmed to be Cash, lived somewhere in the area of the PETCO, Jan created gigantic, florescent poster board signs with a picture of Cash that she plastered all over a good part of the city of Sacramento, centering on a two-mile radius around the store. The signs read, "DID YOU RESCUE THIS DOG ON INTERSTATE 80 ON LABOR DAY?"

Still, there was no response. By the end of the third week, Jan's friends and even her husband were encouraging her to give up. But on the twenty-first day of Cash's hiatus, Jan came home and her husband told her there was a voice mail message that she'd better return right away.

When Jan called the couple from the message, they described Cash to a T, including the fact that Cash had "black spots on his tongue." The couple lived outside the radius where Jan's heavily distributed posters had been hung, but someone who knew them and knew about "their" new dog had seen one and delivered it to them.

When she went to pick up Cash, Jan found that her dog was somewhat confused and suddenly very chubby. It turns out the couple had always owned cats which they "free fed" by keeping a continuous supply of food on the ground. They just assumed this was how you feed a dog, too, and, Cash wasn't about to disagree. It was a good thing Jan "rescued" him back when she did—in just twenty-one days in his new home, Cash had managed to gain twelve pounds!

What I found most fascinating about this story was the behavior of the couple. In an e-mail that she sent me, Jan said that the couple who found Cash, "Had just seen this 'nice dog' by the highway and after rescuing him, decided to keep him. They never considered that someone might actually be looking for him. They never took him to a vet to have him scanned for a microchip, never checked the local paper, Craig's List, or any other place for that matter, for an owner."

Cases like this happen every day, but bound and determined pet owners like Jan Gates, willing to take measures as drastic as finagling her way onto radio airtime and plastering posters all over the city are rare. In her postscript to me, Jan told me she'd also taken a dramatic step to ensure her golden retriever stayed safely at home in the future—since there was no way to fence the Lake Tahoe property, she and her husband sold their cabin and started taking more dog-safe vacations. They didn't want to take a chance that their dog might ever again be "rescued" out of their lives.

Cash was by all accounts an outgoing, friendly dog, and so his pleasing personality was one of the factors that got him taken so quickly into another home. Surprisingly, I discovered that one of the biggest reasons many lost dogs and cats are never returned is a misinterpretation of a different kind of behavior. Animal shelter staff, rescue group volunteers, and dog lovers and cat fanciers often make assumptions about the treatment of dogs and the tameness of cats. When the rescuer finds a lost dog with a skittish, fearful temperament, they typically assume that the dog cowers and acts afraid because it has been abused. Most rescuers in these cases make no attempt to find the owner, even when the dog has a collar with an ID tag. But the behavior that a dog exhibits has very little to do with how the owner treated the dog and everything to do with its individual temperament shaped by genetics, proper socialization, and early-life puppy experiences with littermates. Many dogs are simply hardwired to be skittish and when they become lost, that behavior becomes magnified.

Although feral cats exhibit fearful behavior, so do many domesticated, pet cats that were simply born with a skittish, shy temperament. I discovered that when a lost "scaredy cat" with an easily spooked temperament is found, the rescuer often assumes the reason the cat hisses or runs away in fear is because it's feral. It never occurs to them that the cat hiding under their house could be someone's displaced, panicked, lost housecat.

Fortunately, sometimes the actions of the owner can make a difference. By being sure that the nearby public knows someone's pet is missing and wanted back at home, they can help increase the chances of a safe return.

Flyers with the pet's name, photo, and a mention that the pet is shy can sometimes help alleviate suspicions by the rescuer that the pet has been abused or always lived wild.

Flyers are a valuable tool for handing out to people, but the number one most effective method for recovering pets has proven, time and again, to be giant, neon posters. However, I discovered that in most cases when I gave instructions on how to create proper giant posters, pet owners would often say, "I already did that." And yet when I arrived on location to conduct a search, I'd find that they had not created the large, neon posters but instead simply plastered the area with white, 8 ½ X 11 flyers that were too small to read and virtually unnoticed by passersby.

After reading a book called *Inattentional Blindness*, I discovered the primary reason why large, neon posters work and small, white flyers fail. According to authors Arien Mack and Irvin Rock, there is "no perception without attention." In other words, when something does not grab your attention, you don't perceive it—it's as if the flyer is invisible. Tragically, pet owners who post small flyers that are not even noticed by drivers fail to get the message out that their pet is lost.

To counter this, I launched a campaign called "5+5+55 MPH Rule" which encouraged owners to create big, neon posters using five words that people can read in five seconds if they're driving fifty-five miles per hour. If you were to read the words, "Lost Black Poodle Red Collar" or "Lost Orange Cat Blue Harness" you could visualize what that animal looks like. Convincing pet owners to switch from using flyers to giant, neon colored posters ultimately resulted in the recovery of many missing pets.

Since no one had ever developed a comprehensive system for conducting physical searches for lost pets, I simply continued to use the law enforcement methods that made sense to me. I often wondered why no one had developed this kind of service before, but in the absence of any protocol, I did the best I could with the skills I had. I developed a process that paralleled the way I had conducted lost person investigations.

Each case started with an interview. I compiled a profile of each lost pet, its temperament, the terrain, the circumstance surrounding the search, and any known facts about the pet's disappearance. To keep them straight I assigned each lost-pet incident a case number.

My next step was the law enforcement tactic of conducting a "hasty search"—a rapid, brief search of the high-probability areas. Because I was the only pet detective offering this service, I wanted to be available to work as many cases as possible; I was simply not able to spend days or weeks working on the same lost-pet investigation. Since I was working alone, without a team of volunteers, I was forced to leave the deeper investigative work like surveillance, interviewing neighbors, setting up wildlife cameras and humane traps, and distributing flyers for the pet owners to conduct after I gave them detailed instructions.

Before long, it occurred to me that much of the high-tech equipment I had used in law enforcement could be used in searches for pets, too. One of the first tools I incorporated was the use of the amplified listening device, or ALD. This device is sold in hunting magazines for hunters to detect the movement of game and in police magazines for investigators to use as a surveillance tool. It consists of a plastic parabolic booster that captures and funnels sound into a sensitive microphone. A pair of earphones with a volume control enables miniscule sounds to be amplified. I had previously used this device as a cop when conducting a drug stakeout. It dawned on me that the ALD could detect the meows of a trapped cat and help pinpoint its location.

I also tried using a thermal imaging infrared camera. Used to locate hidden criminals and lost people, this tool detected anything alive that gave off heat. The images in the viewfinder were just like those seen on TV cop shows where helicopters detected fleeing white bloblike criminals. The only drawback was that at the time, the handheld camera cost over twelve thousand dollars, and the company that allowed me to test the device only let me borrow it on special occasions.

On one case, the skinniest of my Half Moon Bay pet detective trainees, Dani Diebert, got her chance to really demonstrate the dedication of a hardworking volunteer when her size made her the only one who could slither into the crawl space under a client's home and use the infrared camera to eliminate the most likely hiding place of the missing cat.

Days later, that cat, named Manuel, was found in one of the other hiding places I had pointed out to its owner. It was the crawl space under the home of a neighbor who had not been available to give permission to search the day we were at the site. That neighbor had replaced the torn screens at the base of their home the day Manuel disappeared—and inadvertently sealed the poor cat in. Manuel was nearly starved to death (and suffered kidney damage) when he was recovered thirty-five days after he disappeared. He had spent five weeks without food and limited rain water and yet lived through his ordeal!

Another device I tested, but also could not afford, was the "Search Cam" camera. Used in disasters to detect humans trapped under rubble, this was a small, articulated camera mounted on the head of a six-foot pole. It had a video screen and control switch on the user end so the user could insert the camera portion under rubble, rotate the camera head 360 degrees, and view the entire area. This was the perfect tool for finding cats hiding or trapped in spaces too small for us to reach. I often thought that tool could have saved the blind Norwich terrier Toby.

But the one tool I used that seemed to some of my friends to be the sign I had gone off the deep end actually opened the door to a whole new angle of lost-pet investigations. It was a case that came down to a matter of positive identification through forensics.

I took a call from Patti Kirby, a woman looking for her lost cat, Cleo. Although I had conducted a few searches by myself, my back still prohibited me from taking cases in areas with rough terrain. Patti's home near the summit of Empire Grade certainly qualified as one I was not ready to tackle.

"I'm sorry," I told her. "But I can't do a search in that area." I explained the situation surrounding my injury and offered to help over the phone if I could. Patti said she had distributed flyers, taken out advertisements, and even developed an announcement for local television. She had turned over every rock and looked in every conceivable distant place for her cat. But when she described Cleo's typical behavior patterns, it seemed unlikely that Cleo had left the area. She did not fit the profile of a cat that would travel far. I told Patti to focus her search close to home.

Then Patti told me there were coyotes in her area. Based on what I had learned from previous searches I told her what to do.

"I'm sorry to have to tell you this," I began, "but you need to look for tufts of fur. Sometimes that's all you'll find at coyote kill-sites. Go out and search again, but this time just look for tufts of fur on the ground."

Two hours later, the phone rang again. It was Patti, this time even more upset.

"I found some tufts of fur," she cried. "They're cream-colored and look like they could belong to Cleo. Can you come out and look at them?"

"Where did you find them?" I asked.

"In the woods down below my cabin," she said. "Not all that far from my place."

"All right," I told her. "I'll make some phone calls and get back to you. Don't touch or move the fur until I get there."

I hung up the phone and called Becky, my eager trainee. She agreed to come with me and said I could pick her up in fifteen minutes.

Finding Cleo alive was unlikely. My goal was to provide an answer for Patti. Especially in cases where the pet was not recovered, I felt I owed it to pet owners to give them a sense of closure. To do this, I needed to find a way to analyze animal fur. I decided that since it was possible to provide positive identifications on hair fibers in law enforcement investigations, there must be a similar way to solve a lost-pet investigation. I knew that it was time to pursue the use of DNA testing.

Thirty minutes later, Becky and I met Patti outside her home. She was in an enclave that separates Santa Cruz County from Santa Clara County. The area was prone to fallen redwood trees, rockslides, power outages, and other such problems during the winter. The people who chose to live in these beautiful but isolated mountains were mostly devoted nature lovers.

Patti led us to the site, where we found several tufts of off-white fur scattered over an area about seven feet in diameter. The ground was covered in leaves, twigs, and redwood scurf, all various shades of brown, black, and tan. If there was any blood in the area, it was concealed in the tapestry of the forest colors. First I wanted to determine whether there was any decomposing blood on the ground.

Becky held Rachel while I instructed her on how to give Rachel the cadaver command.

"Bones," Becky commanded Rachel. "Find Bones." Rachel worked over to the tufts of fur, sniffed the ground, squatted, and peed. Her alert confirmed the presence of blood. Next, we examined the area more closely. I sat motionless for several seconds and watched for insect activity around the hair fibers. I'd long since discovered that flies are physical evidence when searching for a lost pet. I counted three different blowflies, a species of fly that is often found in the presence of human or animal decomposition. They flew away when disturbed and resettled in the same spot when left alone. Something had been killed in this location.

I took my camera and photographed the tufts of fur for my records. Once the photos had been taken, we collected the tufts of fur in a small paper bag and headed back to the cabin.

When we were there, Patti provided a towel, a piece of foam that Cleo slept on, and a few toys, all of which contained strands of Cleo's hair. I collected some of the fur fibers, hoping to find a way to compare them with the kill-site hairs.

"I can't make any promises," I told Patti. "But we'll see if we can do forensic testing on the fur we found."

Prior to my injury, I had given presentations on "Canine Resources for City Searches" at a few child abduction workshops hosted by the California Department of Justice. I had worked directly with two coordinators, Mike Kelly and Olivia Carrera from the Sexual Habitual Offender Program. I was hoping they could refer me to a forensic lab that would analyze cat hair.

When I finally got Mike Kelly on the phone, I was afraid he would laugh at my request. But he didn't. He was enthusiastic and thought my pet detective work was fascinating. Mike gave me the number of a company called Forensic Analytical located in Hayward, California.

"Ask for Michelle Fox," Mike told me. "She's a forensic hair examiner for criminal and civil investigations. She should be able to determine whether the fibers you have are from the cat."

I called Forensic Analytical, wondering what their reaction would be to such a strange request. Michelle Fox, a diehard cat lover, was actually quite interested. But she explained that while she could analyze the hair fibers found at the coyote kill-site and determine what species of animal they came from, she would not be able to make a conclusive comparison of the hair from the kill-site with the confirmed Cleo hairs. Her testing would only identify species, not an individual. The usual cost for a forensic hair examination was more than six hundred dollars. But Michelle agreed to help our nonprofit on a pro bono basis.

We received the results of the forensic examination on August 16, 1998. A portion of Michelle's report read:

> *An examination of the questioned hair from the deceased animal revealed that the hair is consistent with cat hair. A microscopic examination and comparison of the known hairs from Cleo to the questioned hairs from the deceased animal revealed some similarities. Based on these similarities, Cleo can not be excluded as the possible donor of the questioned hairs. It is the opinion of this examiner that the questioned hairs could have come from Cleo.*

We now knew that the tufts of fur belonged to a cat similar to Cleo. But Patti still wanted to know for sure if it *was* Cleo.

"To get that," Michelle told me, "you'll need a DNA test."

Prior to Michelle's forensic hair examination, I was afraid I would be laughed out of law enforcement for requesting forensic tests on pet detective cases. But because of Michelle's cooperation, interest, and professional work on this case, I felt encouraged to move forward and to start calling laboratories that specialized in DNA analysis.

I spoke with Dr. Ann Bowling from the Veterinary Genetics Laboratory at the University of California at Davis. Dr. Bowling told me that extracting DNA from cat hair was certainly possible. She referred me to her assistant, Diane Anderson.

"Yes," Diane responded after hearing my story. "We have worked DNA cases involving dogs and even horses and cattle. We're backlogged on cases right now. It might take us a while, but we can definitely work on your case." I couldn't believe it was so easy. Michelle Fox shipped the Cleo hair samples to U.C. Davis and we waited for the results. A few months later, Dr. Cecilia Penedo, Diane Anderson's associate, called with some bad news.

"The good news is that we were able to extract DNA from the kill-site hair samples," Dr. Penedo told me. "But we couldn't get DNA from the known Cleo hairs. We need a hair fiber that has the follicle attached in order to extract the DNA."

Within a few hours, I was back in Patti's cabin, hunting for another source of Cleo's DNA. Patti had gathered everything in the house that had any Cleo fur or potential DNA. Her collection included a towel, a cat scratching post, a few toys, and two whiskers that Cleo had shed in the cabin.

"Would a cat whisker work?" I asked Dr. Penedo the following morning.

"I really don't know," she said. "Send it in along with the other hair samples and we'll give it a try." I packed the materials and shipped them off that afternoon. When I filled out the form at UPS, I had to write down on the shipping list what I was shipping. I wondered what the UPS carrier would think when he or she read that the package contained, "cat hair and cat whiskers."

The call I had been waiting for came six weeks later.

It was Dr. Penedo. "We have a match!"

I was elated that the technique had worked. But I dreaded the phone call I would have to make to Patti. "Was it the whisker?"

"You got it," Dr. Penedo said. "We weren't sure if we could extract DNA from a whisker. We had never tried it before so one of our technicians brought in a whisker from her cat at home. We experimented with that and extracted DNA. Then we tested Cleo's whisker and successfully extracted her DNA. Cleo's DNA was a perfect match to the kill-site DNA."

"Thank you so much for your help," I told Dr. Penedo. "It really means a lot to me and to Cleo's owner."

We posted the results of the DNA analysis on our Web site. A portion of the final report from Dr. Penedo read:

> *DNA types obtained from a single root of whisker hair are identical to those obtained from hair roots obtained from fur collected at kill-site. Based on DNA identity in 12 microsatellite DNA markers, it is our conclusion that the two samples are from a single individual identified as CLEO.*

It was a bittersweet moment when I called and broke the news to Patti. Whether it was a testament to her hopeful nature or her unwillingness to accept the fact that the cat she deeply loved like a child was gone, she refused to believe the match meant that Cleo was dead. It was, after all, just hair. We had never actually found her cat. But I knew beyond all doubt that everything I could do to solve this case had already been done. The final closure was dependent on time, acceptance, and how long it would take for Patti's heart to heal.

Chapter Thirteen

CAT TRAILS

It was one of the great learning curves of my formative months as a pet detective to discover that the vast majority of people who lose a cat search in all the wrong places and in all the wrong ways. Most pet owners imagine their missing cat is blocks, or even miles, away, but I found that most missing cats seldom left their territory (willingly) or the immediate vicinity of their homes.

In learning about lost cat behavior, I had help from the least likely source in my household: my own independent-to-a-fault cat, Yogi.

As far as I'd been able to tell over the nine years I had taken care of Yogi, she was happily unconcerned about any other creature on the planet (except for mice). She rarely acknowledged the dogs or me, and when guests or neighbors were inside my home, they would have been hard-pressed to notice there was a cat in the vicinity at all. Yogi made a habit of just disappearing. Her outdoor adventures took place long before I became convinced that the best way to truly care for a cat is to keep it indoors 24/7.

In her travels, Yogi studiously avoided the road that passed in front of my cabin for safer routes. She worked her way along the north side in an ivy patch territory that spanned a mere fifty-yard circumference and she *always* kept to that side of the road.

So the morning I came out my front door and saw Yogi crouched in the middle of the road a hundred yards away, I thought I was looking at someone else's orange cat. Since she was afraid of the road, being hunkered down near the double yellow line was the *last* place I expected to find her. The first thing that came to mind was that she must have found a mouse or a rat that had lost its daring race across the road. Maybe her inner hunter craving for rodents had outweighed her hard-earned common sense. But as I strained my eyes, I couldn't see anything else in the roadway.

Early that evening, I received a call from my friend and neighbor Andrea Elliott. Her house was at the top of the hill and on the south side of the street, overlooking my tiny cabin.

"Have you seen Rocky?" Andrea asked. Andrea had four cats and all of them were black-and-white shorthairs. I wasn't exactly sure which cat was Rocky.

"No," I said. "Does he ever come down here?"

"He goes all over," Andrea answered. "I let him out this morning and haven't seen him since. This is really unusual for him. He's always home for dinner." Andrea knew she was talking to a pet detective. What she didn't know was that I had seen behavior in Yogi that I began to suspect could be related to Rocky's disappearance.

"I'll bring Rachel out so we can start checking the neighborhood," I told Andrea. "Meet me down on Conference Drive. There's something in the road that I want to have Rachel check out."

I harnessed Rachel, grabbed the amplified listening device and headed out the door. We didn't have a lot of daylight left, and I wanted to get going. I headed toward the patch of roadway where Yogi had been sniffing earlier in the day. Andrea walked down her driveway and met me in the road as I began to scan the ground for any spots of blood.

"Yogi was sniffing at something in the center of the road this morning," I explained. "If there is any blood or animal scent in the roadway, Rachel will alert by urinating." I really didn't need to explain this to Andrea. She had listened to many of my pet detective stories over pasta and wine dinners on my deck and knew all about Rachel's unconventional training.

"Bones," I commanded Rachel. I directed her to start checking scents near the yellow double lines. Rachel worked approximately five yards, then focused on a scent in the roadway. After sniffing for several seconds, Rachel squatted and urinated. I examined the roadway and discovered a faint, white streak that was approximately eighteen inches long.

"What is that?" I asked out loud as I tried to understand what I was looking at. "It almost looks like a line of chalk." I knelt down and looked closely at the streak as Rachel strained to sniff it. It was then that I noticed tiny black-and-white clumps of fur were attached to portions of the streak. Later we determined that the white streak was actually the result of a bone being ground into the pavement as the cat was dragged by a car. Immediately, I knew that we were looking for an injured cat, not one that had just wandered away.

Andrea and I began a frantic search of the area using Rachel and the amplified listening device. Andrea lived on the south side of the roadway, but it appeared Rocky had been hit on the north side. I assumed that he would have run downhill, north, off into the woods on the same side of the road where he was hit. We conducted a limited search on the north side, primarily around my cabin, but it was dark by then and the terrain was too steep for my still-uncooperative back. I would need to make a few phone calls to find a volunteer who could come and search the area the following day.

"I'm going to leave the listening device with you," I told Andrea. I felt like I was letting her down since I could not work the steep, ivy-covered terrain where we thought Rocky could be. "Call me if you need anything."

The following morning, Andrea stopped by with news.

"I found him at five this morning," she told me. "He was under my front porch. He tried to hop away from me, but I was able to grab him. His leg was in terrible shape."

"Is he all right?" I asked.

"They are amputating his leg," Andrea said sadly. "The vet says that he should recover, though, and that cats can learn to get around on three legs almost as well as on four. I can't believe that he was out there and wouldn't meow when I called him."

In spite of the fact that he had been hit by a car on the north side of the road and the easiest direction would have been to run north, Rocky instead had crawled south toward his home. He had navigated straight up a steep incline through brush in order to hide in his own territory. And he had refused to meow in response to our calls.

Rocky's behavior heightened my interest. Thinking about my own cat Yogi, I remembered that she had behaved in the same way. Two years prior, Yogi had vanished after being injured and dragged herself under my neighbor's deck. In spite of the fact that I had called her for several days and even looked under that deck, Yogi had not made a sound. And, not surprisingly,

Yogi had crawled under the deck at the same spot where I later discovered the stick with the high-probability cat-hair evidence.

Because of Rocky, I had stumbled across another pattern of behavior. Many of the outdoor-access cats that we'd found deceased were found in their outdoor litterbox. When injured, cats will run to an area of concealment that is familiar to them. I looked back at my records of all the injured and deceased cats I had found. In the sixteen cases of injured or deceased cats, ninety percent were found within a *one-house radius* of their owner's home. Sixty-three percent of these cats were not killed instantly. This meant that while these cats were injured and in need of veterinary care, their owners were spending their time and efforts printing up lost-cat fliers and driving to the animal shelter. It never occurred to these owners that their cats, like Rocky and Yogi, might be nearby and hiding in silence.

"I just can't believe he was right there," Andrea said again the next day when I called to check on Rocky's condition. "He could have died under my own porch."

In an amazingly short amount of time, Rocky recovered from his surgery. He reclaimed his territory, but he was no longer indistinguishable among Andrea's collection of black-and-white shorthairs. I was grateful that Rocky had opened my eyes to what became one of the core premises of lost-cat recovery: search close to home (within the cat's territory) and do *not* expect the cat to meow in response to calls.

Once I was aware of most cats' propensity for sticking close to home when they were missing, it opened up a whole new realm of possibility for searching. I was able to offer useful advice to some clients without even leaving home. Over a two-year period, I collected data on lost-cat behavior. Through resources over the Internet, I distributed lost-cat surveys and asked questions of pet owners who had previously lost cats. I ended up with a drawer full of data and enough information to expand on my cat-profiling ideas. Over time, I was able to examine an individual lost-cat incident and develop a profile, applying percentages to indicate what likely happened to the cat.

Most cases led me directly back to conducting an aggressive search within a three-house radius of the lost cats' territory and to discoveries that enabled me to add to the list of behaviors I came to expect from lost cats.

One was what I called the "silence factor"—the fact that sick cats, injured cats (like Yogi and Rocky), and panicked cats typically did not give any audible response when their owners called them. Walking around calling "Here, kitty, kitty" proved to be a resoundingly ineffective way of searching.

One couple, who recovered their cat due to my e-mail instructions, discovered the ineffectiveness of calling a lost-cat. Another Rocky, also an outdoor-access cat, vanished from his home in Snohomish, WA. His family, Gary and Jennifer, conducted the typical search that involved calling their cat by name, posting flyers in the neighborhood, and checking the shelters. They contacted me through our Web site after Rocky had been missing for seven days. Gary and Jennifer took my advice and obtained permission from their neighbors to carefully search their yards. In a testimonial they submitted for our Web site, here's how they found Rocky:

> *We took to heart your "1-3 house radius" and went out looking again closer to home for our outdoor-access cat, Rocky. We finally found our precious Rocky and it was none too soon. We found him 2 houses away in a backyard, behind a shed, 20 feet into blackberry brambles wrapped up in barbed-wire. We had both been in the area before, close enough to hear him and him to hear us, but we believe he was in silent mode. This time he talked back so we could crawl in & locate him. We suffered several wounds getting to him but nothing like he sustained. He tried so hard to get free of the barbed-wire he pulled skin off. This injury is pretty severe, but he is going to make it. Rocky also lost a lot of weight, was severely dehydrated, caught a respiratory infection, and developed a heart murmur. We know he got caught up the first day he disappeared or he would have come home, so he was in there for seven days. He is still in the hospital but will make it. We want to thank you for your email and words of encouragement. We feel we never would have found him without your advice and helpful suggestions.*

Another pattern of behavior I discovered was that when escaped indoor-only cats were first recovered, many continued their evasive behavior, often behaving as if their owners were total strangers—as much like feral cats as those who had lived on their own all their lives. Fortunately, after a few days back home, even the most dramatically changed cat usually recovered its previous, tamer personality.

Knowing that many lost cats hunker down nearby and aren't necessarily in any hurry to get home led me to a new strategy for recovering them. It dawned on me one day that a piece of equipment already used in the pet industry for getting *rid* of cats could be used to recover them. The humane trap, a rectangle-shaped wire cage customarily set up by folks trying to capture feral cats and either take them to an animal shelter or neuter and return them to a feral cat colony, turned out to be the perfect tool to recover a lost cat.

In conducting my research into lost-pet behaviors, I noticed there was virtually no information on the Internet or in books that addressed the issue. For example, there was no term used to describe the behavior in which indoor-only cats hide near the escape point in silence. So I called this factor "displacement" and started using that term widely. I also began to develop protocols for how to search for a displaced (indoor-only escaped) cat verses how to search for an outdoor-access cat that had suddenly vanished. Most lost-pet Web sites at the time did not address any difference between displaced cats and missing outdoor-access cats.

I discovered that panicked cats, sick cats, cats in unfamiliar territory, or cats that are terrified by an event that disrupts their territory, such as an earthquake or fireworks, will avoid human contact, hide nearby, and remain silent. The longer the cat remains in that place, the more scent it deposits there. Ultimately, that safe hiding spot becomes the cat's new territory. If food is placed inside a humane trap, though, the cat can be recovered and returned home.

This discovery enabled me to help recover lost cats without my needing to be present. In one week in particular, I received four phone calls about four different lost indoor-only cats who had escaped outdoors. First there was Chester, whose owner had no earthly idea how he got outside. Then there was Jerry, who bolted from a plastic crate to avoid a trip to the veterinarian. Next came Moosie, who pushed out a window screen to gain her freedom. And lastly, I heard from a friend of mine, Marsha Bates, who called right after her cat Tigger slipped out between the legs of the mailman when Marsha opened the door to sign for a package. In all four cases, I recommended that the owners borrow a humane trap and use it as a recovery tool. Within eight days, *all four* cats were trapped and recovered by their owners. In Tigger's case, Marsha didn't know where to set the humane trap so I told her to set it on her porch. When she checked the trap thirty minutes later, a grumpy Tigger was inside, sour that his newfound freedom had been so quickly terminated.

By giving cat owners simple trapping instructions, I began to see case after case in which an indoor-only cat that had escaped outdoors was returned home, sometimes even *months* after the cat had escaped. However, I ran into an unexpected problem. Many of the animal shelters I referred cat owners to so they could rent or borrow a humane trap would not allow the traps to be used for this purpose. As crazy as this sounds, many shelters were willing to allow their officers and the public to use the traps to capture feral cats, but they had no policy in place to allow the public to borrow these traps to capture a lost housecat. It was simply unheard of at the time, creating a difficult barrier for cat owners to overcome.

I recall a case that still haunts me to this day. A professor from Arizona called me, begging me to bring my bloodhound to Phoenix to help her track her missing cats. She and her husband had been involved in a horrendous rollover car accident in the desert in which her three cats were thrown from the car. Her husband was in critical condition in the hospital and the professor, injured herself, was in desperate need of someone who could offer her hands-on help. Even though her cats were crated, their plastic carriers had all broken open in the crash, sending the cats running in terror into the desert.

I was not available to travel to Arizona to help her. I encouraged her to contact feral-cat groups in the Phoenix area to see if someone, anyone, would be willing to humanely trap her three cats. Even though using humane traps to recover lost cats was unheard of at that time, I knew that feral cat groups had the equipment and the trapping experience to be able to recover these cats. Sadly, not one of the groups she contacted was willing to respond and help her. The cats were never found.

Thankfully, in my endeavor to make cat owners aware of the big help that comes in the form of a humane trap, I received valuable and unexpected assistance from a missing cat named Sage and her owner, Pauline Phung.

Sage was a nine-year-old purebred Russian blue shorthaired cat who escaped from her San Jose home. Pauline saw Sage push open a window screen and jump out into her front yard. Pauline tried to gently coax Sage back inside but the cat was so frightened she bolted and darted into a neighbor's yard. As Pauline combed the area and called for her cat, Sage was nowhere to be found.

One of the first questions I ask when profiling a cat is how it behaves with strangers. Eventually, in cases of less skittish cats, I was able to coach the owners in how to use their house as a trap. This method involves the use of bait, a driveway alarm set outside their front door, and perfect timing. When done correctly, a cat can be lured back into their own home without the use of a humane trap. The owner hides inside behind the door and, after hearing the beep of the driveway alarm, quickly shuts the door after the cat has entered, essentially catching the cat in the house.

When I profiled Sage, I learned that she was skittish and shy. Pauline said that when a stranger came into her home, Sage would run and hide underneath a bed. The fact that Sage was a "scaredy cat" (even inside her own home) was an indication that she would be a very panicked kitty when she found herself in unfamiliar territory.

Pauline was worried because she hadn't heard about any sightings from her neighbors. Sage seemed to have just disappeared. The logical assumption was that her cat had run away, but I encouraged Pauline to believe that Sage was actually hiding close by. I told Pauline that the fact that no one had seen Sage was normal. Indoor-only cats that escape outdoors are seldom seen by anyone because they are adept at hiding. Sage would probably only leave her hiding place during the stillness of night when there was limited noise and human activity. She would likely sneak out to find a source of food or water and then dart right back into her hiding place—usually under a deck, porch, or shed or inside heavy brush.

My first recommendation to Pauline was that she use a baited humane trap to try to capture Sage. Cats can hide in silence for days, even weeks. I had noticed one particular pattern of behavior in many cases, though, that I called the "threshold factor," and it was a theory that I was able to use to give hope to distraught cat owners who thought that each passing day meant a reduced chance of finding the cat. In these cases, certain cats hid in the same spot for seven to fourteen days before they finally decided to meow and make their location known.

The only way I could explain the threshold factor was to speculate that it often took seven to fourteen days for most domestic, well-fed cats to reach the point (threshold) where they simply couldn't stand it anymore. I can envision a panicked cat, hiding for days, until it becomes so hungry, so thirsty, that it listens to its owner call its name for the millionth time and finally, the kitty figures something like, *This is stupid...I'm hungry, I'm thirsty. I'm ready to go home now. "Meerrrrroooooowww."*

Pauline was willing to get a humane trap, but she was more interested in knowing if I could respond with a search dog. I responded along with one of my Half Moon Bay volunteers, Sheryl Carver, and her dog Leo, a cat-detection dog in training. We made a systematic search of the area. We started with Sage's yard and found there were virtually no hiding places there. We progressed into other yards and found a few that had significant areas of heavy foliage, mini junkyards, and berry vines that created places we could not access. In those yards, I advised Pauline to place a baited humane trap.

Unfortunately, we ran into a roadblock in the search for Sage that is all too common in pet searches, but unheard of in searches for lost people. One neighbor refused to let us search on his property. In police work, this would be an incredibly unlikely response from a neighbor, and easily surmountable. In police work, I had used my search dogs in exigent circumstances when searching for missing persons or for criminals who would elude capture should I have to wait for a search warrant. Thus, in police searches, I had the authority and luxury of going on private property or anywhere that my search dog led me. But in searches for lost pets, it is a sad fact of life that not everyone is willing to open a gate or allow a physical search of their private property.

When I left that day, I advised Pauline to keep working with her traps and not give up hope. A healthy cat can survive, sometimes indefinitely, on its own, and since she had no reason to suspect an injury and no knowledge of predators in the area, Sage had a good chance of making it.

I didn't hear from Pauline for a week, but on week two, she sent me an e-mail and asked a few questions. She told me she had purchased two humane traps—one that she moved around the neighborhood and another that she kept baited in her back yard. I was happy to hear she was sticking with it. Two more weeks passed and I had not heard from Pauline. I assumed that, like most cat owners, Pauline had given up.

But she hadn't. Twenty-seven days after Sage had escaped from her home, Pauline got her kitty back. Sage entered the baited trap in Pauline's back yard and was safely caught inside. Pauline had faithfully baited the trap every night in hopes that Sage would come home. Sage was dehydrated and had lost several pounds, but she was alive and Pauline was elated to have her back. Within two weeks, Sage had begun to regain the lost weight and had settled back into her normal routine at home.

Another pet detective tool that came after the Sage case that quickly proved to be highly successful in recovering skittish, hard-to-catch cats (and dogs) was the digital wildlife camera. Although these cameras were widely used by hunters and wildlife biologists, no one in the pet rescue community was using them at the time. However, we immediately had success when setting up wildlife cameras at lost pet feeding stations. In cases of displaced, indoor-only cats that had escaped outside we discovered that we could set out a plate of food with a wildlife camera and use it to confirm that the cat was hiding near that location. Once we captured the cat on camera, we'd then replace the plate of food with a baited humane trap and capture the cat within days, sometimes hours.

Sage and Pauline's case plus the inclusion of digital wildlife cameras demonstrated again that my search dogs were not the only solution to the lost-pet problem. I was relieved to find that there were ways I could help locate pets without going out and physically investigating each case. I was just one person, in one city, with a doozy of a bad back, and it was impossible for me to help everyone. I dreaded the times when I took calls from distraught pet owners and had to tell them I could not come search.

Thankfully, in helping pet owners over the phone and Internet, I began to share my findings about lost-pet behavior every chance I got. As a result, I started to help pet owners who were states—even continents—away. I once helped a man from Croatia whose cat had jumped out a second story window. The man had searched all over his neighborhood but could not find his cat. He located my Web site, read the information on lost-cat behavior, went back outside, and began to look in hiding places. Minutes later, he found his cat hiding in a space between two walls. He quickly extricated her, bundled her up, and carried her back upstairs to his apartment where she belonged. I was elated every time a cat owner wrote or called to tell me my Web site advice helped them find their missing cat.

One of my favorite long-distance cases came in the form of a young woman who had attended one of the "Lost Cat Behavior" seminars that I presented at a national animal welfare conference. Emily planned to use the information she learned to help others find their lost cats and had taken careful note of what she would do herself if her own cat ever got lost. Her absolute confidence in my methods was flattering, and the results were pretty incredible. This is what Emily wrote in the e-mail that she sent: "Using the information I learned from you, it took me two minutes or less to find my friend's missing cat. I wish I had had a stopwatch."

Emily's friend's cat Tiger had been missing for three days, and the friend had given up hope, but Emily was sure she could track down the missing cat. Upon arriving on the scene, an apartment in an urban area, she looked around and saw only one viable hiding place in the immediate vicinity: a patch of bushes at the end of the apartment building, bordering the parking lot. With a bag of treats, a humane trap, a friend, and the wheelchair-bound, worried cat owner in tow, Emily approached the bushes and found exactly what she was expecting to see: Tiger, looking panicked, hunkered down and waiting to be rescued.

The cat's owner helped coax Tiger from his hiding place and they were able to go home together.

Emily wrote that another well-meaning friend of the cat owner had been so sure Tiger would not be found that she'd gone ahead and adopted a kitten to replace him. In the end, the problem was not getting over the loss of one pet; it was how she was going to care for two.

Lost cats like Tiger hide in silence all of the time. And just like Tiger's mom, cat owners prematurely terminate their search efforts all of the time. One of the most common reasons cat owners stop searching is they mistakenly assume that their cat was killed by a coyote. While coyotes do kill cats in certain communities, they just do *not* kill and consume them on the level that most people fear.

Missing cats don't just vanish into thin air—the majority of them end up in feral cat colonies or in animal shelters where they are never claimed. One of the primary reasons why these "stray" cats go unclaimed is not because they are not loved or missed, but because by the time they overcome their fear and allow themselves to be captured, several weeks or months have passed. The families who once loved these cats gave up long ago, often replacing their missing cat with another one just like nearly happened with Tiger. One of the goals I set about to achieve was to educate animal shelter workers in principles of lost-cat and displaced-cat behaviors. I am convinced that many feline lives could be saved if shelter workers understood how lost cats behave and if they shared that information with the public.

I guess it's true what they say about not being able to understand someone until you have walked a mile in their shoes. It was not until I had spent years studying and searching for lost cats that I began to have an appreciation of the way they behave. But once I did, that little bit of understanding grew into a deeper affection. I was an avid dog lover. And while I had always had cats, I never felt particularly close to any of them.

Since her valuable, if unintentional, help in finding Andrea's cat Rocky, Yogi had picked up right where she left off in our relationship. If I picked her up to cuddle, Yogi would stiffen, squirm, and push her body away in a frantic effort to break free. She was one of the most aloof creatures I had ever met.

After hearing countless cat lovers gush about the sweet nature of their cats, I began to realize my crabby cat, Yogi, had duped me. I had assumed that all cats were aloof like her. Once I realized that sweet-natured cats existed, I decided that my little family—now comprised of me, my three dogs, and Yogi—needed another cat. And that's how I found myself at the Santa Cruz SPCA one afternoon, looking longingly at the kittens, trying to narrow my choice down to just one.

The kitten room was encased in glass, and as I watched several kitties play and bat at toys, and each other, one little gray-and-white kitty caught my eye. He was a skinny little boy, with an unusual E.T.-shaped face and an exotic look. As soon as I stepped inside the room, he leapt from the towering cat tree that he had conquered down into my arms. I was taken aback: not by his gregarious nature, but by his fleas. He also had a runny nose and was sneezing.

I wanted a healthy, happy kitten and not a flea-bitten, sick, scrawny one. Yet as he nuzzled his cold, wet, little burnt-orange-colored nose up to my face and with his raspy, sandpaper tongue licked my own nose, I knew I was in trouble—so I set him down and tried to walk away.

"I really don't want to take a sick cat home," I said, knowing how highly contagious an upper respiratory infection can be. The last thing I needed was to make Yogi sick or incur more vet bills.

"We'll send him home with antibiotics," the shelter volunteer answered as she picked him up and thrust him back into my arms.

"I really don't want to have to deal with fleas," I argued.

"All you have to do is treat him with some topical flea medication," she replied. The kitten snuggled his head up under my chin.

"But," I pushed on, as the kitten started to purr, "won't the fleas jump off onto my other pets?"

"Not if you take him straight to your vet," the shelter worker said. She took two steps back so that I couldn't pass the kitten back to her.

I said something to the effect of "put a ribbon on him," and I watched as the volunteer loaded him in a cardboard cat carrier box (I had left my own cat carrier at home, not intending to make yet another hasty decision about a pet) and carried my new, flea-infested, respiratory-infected precious kitten out the door.

It took just a few hours (post-veterinary visit) for my new kitten to adjust to his new housemates. Rachel nuzzled and licked and became best buddies with the little gray wonder. I named him "Myron" because, well, he just looked like a Myron. He had bright eyes and a cute little scowling expression on his face. His dark gray, striped fur on his body and face contrasted with the white fur on his cheeks and chin, giving him an appearance a bit like a bunny. Myron would cuddle and sleep on my lap, even wrap his warm, soft belly around my neck like a scarf that kept me warm when I was working at my computer.

When he was four months old, I decided to promote Myron from his job of lap cat and neck-warmer to that of "target cat." I had two volunteers with new cat-detection dogs that I was training, and we needed a kitty that would tolerate dogs. Since Myron loved Rachel so much, I wanted to use him as the cat I would crate and hide. This would require that I teach Myron to lay quietly and happily inside a crate.

In addition to hiding in a crate, I wanted to be able to use Myron to lay a scent trail by taking him for a walk. Because he was going to be an indoor-only cat, I needed to train Myron to walk with me while wearing a harness attached to a long lead. Myron resisted at first, but quickly became adjusted to wearing his tiny nylon harness and to walking outdoors while attached to me. When I mentioned to Shannon, the veterinary technician at Dr. Miller's office, that I was "harness training" Myron, she mistook his new skill for a sign that he was going into the family business. She associated "harness" with my bloodhound tracking services. Mystified, Shannon looked at Myron, then at me, then at Myron again and asked, "So, you're training this cat *to search for lost dogs?"*

"Not this year," I laughed. "But you never know!"

Myron was, to say the least, a good sport about it all, and by the time my precious "target cat" reached his first birthday, I was amazed I hadn't been a cat lover all my life. My scowly kitty had converted me completely.

Chapter Fourteen
ABOUT AN AIREDALE

When I answered the call about a missing Airedale, I could hear the panic in the caller's voice. I'd become accustomed to hearing a certain amount of alarm in my clients' tones—a combination of worry about their lost pets, fear that it might already be too late to find them, and a little anxiety about the fact that they were desperately enlisting the help of a pet detective in their hour of need, even when they weren't quite sure what a pet detective could do.

But Bob Pyle, who wanted his dog, George, found ASAP, had yet another legitimate reason for concern: He shared custody of the dog with his girlfriend. She was away at a family reunion. Bob had been entrusted with George's care. He needed to get his dog back fast.

"When did you last see George?" I asked, taking notes in the search log I kept by the phone.

"Yesterday morning," he answered. "I put him out in the pasture beside my house while I ran errands."

An Airedale in a fenced field—I shook my head at the thought. This is the biggest of the terriers, an intelligent, independent breed to begin with, and a breed that I'd never known to take confinement lying down. It is the last breed of dog, besides a bloodhound, of course, I'd expect to hear had been put out to pasture and stayed there.

"What have you done already?" I needed to know.

"I've searched the property and looked around my neighbors' houses, too, but this is a pretty rural area with a lot of open spaces. I called the animal shelter, and they told me I could call this number," he explained. "Do you think you could come out and have your dog search for George?"

Before I could answer, he continued, "My girlfriend will be back tomorrow night. Do you think you can find him before then?"

Finding George on miles of coastal farmland sounded like a challenge. Finding him with the specter of an angry co-owner's return hanging over my head didn't appeal to me one bit. But it was obvious as Bob went on about his dog that stubborn, Houdini-esque George was a much-loved member of the family and Bob had run out of resources for finding him.

I knew that if I didn't help him, no one would. So I told him I would try.

This was a rural search in an area halfway between Hollister, an agricultural community, and Monterey, a beautiful, ritzy tourist town next to the Pacific Ocean. Hollister is known for its fruit; Monterey for its otters floating on kelp beds, cracking open oysters on their tummies as they lie on their backs. Thankfully, this search wasn't in the Santa Cruz Mountains and I didn't need to worry about steep terrain. The area consisted of flat pastures of lettuce, artichokes, and strawberries and scattered cherry and apricot orchards. The flat ground meant I could handle the dogs myself and didn't need to rely upon having a volunteer available. I told Bob I'd be there within an hour.

On the day of this search, my trusty tracking partner A.J. was out of commission due to an undiagnosed limp. When I realized that I needed another trailing dog—a *good* trailing dog in addition to Rachel—I turned to Chase. It was time to see what she was made of.

I had used Chase on a few previous missing-pet cases, but not many. As a puppy, she had exhibited fear-based dog aggression—kind of a get-them-before-they-get-you philosophy toward other dogs. Because of this, working her was often a challenge. While my underused supersleuth had superior drive and determination to track the scent of a dog, I needed to make sure Chase never quite *got* to the dog. After all, this was supposed to be search-and-*rescue* and not search-and-*destroy!* But I was confident that her grumpy behavior could be managed and that her misdirected eagerness to hunt down another dog could be harnessed into helping rescue another dog.

It was a foggy day when I pulled into Bob's circular dirt, driveway. His ranch, which included a barn with horses and neighbors who owned a few goats and sheep, was situated in an area dotted with fruit orchards and a few vegetable fields. Bob heard my truck pull in and met me outside. Before I unloaded the dogs, I wanted to survey the area. Bob told me that George had been confined to a horse pasture behind his home. The bottom portion of the pasture fencing was lined with a "hot wire" that carried an electrical current. Under normal circumstances, George would have received a slight electrical zap if he had tried to crawl under the fence. But the electrical current had not been on and George had easily crawled through the fence and walked away.

My first priority was to determine the precise point where George escaped. This would help establish the direction of travel and eliminate searching in the wrong direction. Bob pointed out three possible escape points: under the north barbed-wire fence, through the east gate into the neighbor's pasture, or under a stall door of the barn that led to the front yard on the south side. The only way to determine the correct direction of travel was to trust the work of my dogs.

When I opened the back of my truck, Chase greeted me with her comical "wooooo, wooooo, wooooo" (they always came in threes) which she usually saved for when she wanted something from me. Rachel, on the other hand, lived up to her nickname of "whiner-amer," because she was standing in her crate, whining with impatience. Both dogs were saying "Me first! Me first!" as best they could. Since Rachel was the tried-and-true veteran, I decided to work her first.

My strategy was to eliminate the wrong areas until my dogs indicated the correct route of travel. I would start with the exit from the barn door that led into the front yard. I had Bob bring out the sheepskin rug that George normally slept on and set it on the front lawn just beyond the barn door. I harnessed Rachel and brought her up to the rug.

"Take scent," I commanded Rachel as I lifted the fluffy rug to her nose. "Search!" Rachel gave a quick sniff and began to search. She pulled into the harness and began sniffing and snooping around the yard. She then jogged out the driveway and started east on the dirt road that led to Bob's house. Rachel went about twenty yards, stopped, and turned herself around. This meant there was no George-scent heading east toward the foothills. Rachel stayed on the dirt road and trotted west, passing George's home, but after only going about fifty yards, she stopped and turned back toward the house. There was no scent heading west either.

"I don't think he left from the front yard," I told Bob. "She's indicating his scent isn't here. Let's go check the exit point from the north side of the pasture."

The exit point I was referring to was located on busy Fairview Road. Bob told me that if George had crawled under the barbed-wire fence on the north pasture, he would have been confined in a tiny fenced alleyway that ran parallel along his back fence line. The only escape point from that alleyway would have been to head west and come out onto the road. We walked out onto the two-lane roadway heading toward the alleyway. As we got close, I noticed a fresh set of skid marks in the northbound lane on Fairview Road.

"These skid marks could mean George was hit by a car," I pointed out to Bob, thinking that this was getting to be an all-too-familiar theme in my searches. The case of Andrea's cat Rocky was still very fresh in my memory.

"I guess it's possible," Bob said, "but there are so many cars that travel fast on this road that the skid marks could be from anything." I couldn't argue. Although it was a country road with minimal amount of traffic, the cars were passing by at speeds that I estimated to be between fifty to sixty miles per hour.

We arrived at the alleyway, which was a grassy area fenced in on all four sides. There was an opening at the bottom of the wire fence large enough for a dog to squeeze under. Once there was a break in traffic, I commanded Rachel to search.

Immediately, Rachel began to work a scent trail. I could tell by the intensity in her body language that it was a good, strong scent she was on. She leaned hard in the harness, dragging me with determination. She began to work north, but indicated the scent stopped and that she wanted to cross the street—right near where the skid marks ended. We crossed the roadway and immediately Rachel began to work a scent trail heading south along the west side of Fairview Road. We worked south for about a quarter of a mile and then cut into a cherry orchard. Rachel worked a short distance into the orchard, zigging and then zagging, but eventually she lost the scent.

At some point behind us we had missed a turn. The cherry trees were in full bloom and although I savored the sweet aroma, I suspected that the pungent scent had interfered with my dogs' olfactory abilities. My job was to turn around and, relying on Rachel's body language, determine the spot where George had turned. But after several attempts to get Rachel back into the scent, I gave up. It was time to work Chase.

Before I started Chase at the alleyway, I wanted to see what she would do in front of George's house. Would she confirm Rachel's work? Would she follow Rachel's scent, or do as she was trained and only follow George's scent? I flipped the sheepskin rug over and scented Chase on the opposite side from where Rachel had sniffed.

"Search!" I commanded my beautiful bloodhound. Full of wrinkles and spunk, Chase's chestnut-colored coat often reflected a hint of a reddish-copper color when exposed to direct sunlight. Besides being a fantastic-looking dog, Chase was a blast to work. She pulled so hard in the harness with such drive and determination that she nearly yanked me off my feet. Chase worked with her nose plastered on the ground and was very easy to read. When she lost a scent, she would lift her nose off the ground, shake her entire body and turn herself around. But unlike A.J., who usually made eye contact with me and kept his head held high, Chase would simply put her nose back down and start hunting for scent heading in another direction.

Like Rachel, Chase trotted east along the dirt road in front of Bob's house. But she only tracked for fifteen feet when she stopped, shook herself off, and turned around. She had stopped shorter than Rachel had gone, so that told me Chase probably was not tracking Rachel's scent. She was determined to get to the dog whose scent was on the blanket. Chase began jogging west along the same dirt roadway heading toward Fairview Road. She dipped north into the next-door neighbor's driveway, which was an area that Rachel had not gone into. This confirmed she was not tracking Rachel. Chase only worked about twenty yards west along the dirt road when she shook off and indicated there was no more George scent.

Both dogs had eliminated the dirt road as an exit point. This meant that we could eliminate the neighborhood and foothills east of Bob's home. Now we needed to see if Chase would confirm the scent trail that Rachel had worked. Bob followed behind as I led Chase on the narrow shoulder along Fairview Road.

Because the roadway shoulder was narrow and the occasional cars whooshed by us so fast, we had to walk inside a trash-littered, hollow depression of a dry ditch that ran along the east side of the road. As we exited the ditch and walked up to the grass alleyway, I had Chase by the collar. She began pulling and straining to smell something at the fence line. I let go of her collar. She put her nose directly on the lush green grass that covered the ground at the base of the wire fence. She snuffled in rapid succession, scanning her nose and floppy jowls back and forth along one spot of grass. I had only seen this type of intense sniffing on a few occasions—it was when she picked up the scent of another dog. Chase was sniffing the grass right where George would have rubbed with his tummy if he had crawled out from under the wire alleyway fence.

"Search!" I commanded, knowing that Chase would understand I wanted her to follow the scent of that dog. Since Rachel had not even gone up to the base of the fence, I was confident it was George's scent that my bloodhound was locked onto. Thankfully there was no traffic, because Chase shot like a bullet west across the dangerous Fairview Road and began pulling me south along its west edge, the same route Rachel had taken.

Chase worked down into the same cherry orchard that Rachel had worked, but continued working past the point where Rachel had stopped. It was difficult navigating the dry, crusty ridges and dips. The up-and-down and up-and-down-again terrain within the rows and rows of cherry trees played havoc on my knees and my back. The ground was dry and solid in the low-lying areas but the ridges consisted of giant dirt clods that shifted or buckled and nearly tripped me when I walked on them. But I knew enough about searching through orchards to appreciate the dryness of the ground. Working through a freshly plowed orchard would be even worse.

Because one row of cherry trees looked just like the other, it was easy to get turned around and not be sure which row we had just come from. Chase tracked an additional quarter mile, cut west, and ended up on a dirt roadway deep within the orchard.

The only problem, as I quickly figured out, was that Chase had missed a turn somewhere in the maze of trees and we were now out of scent. We retraced our steps and spent about a half hour trying to pick up the scent again, but it was no use—the primary scent in the orchard was cherry blossoms and not Airedales. The most I could do was to tell Bob that George had left south from his home through the orchard and that he should focus his search heading in that direction.

We returned to his home in silence. I loaded the dogs in my truck. Bob was very appreciative but clearly disappointed that we had not found George. He didn't know how he was going to break the news to his girlfriend. She would be devastated. I have learned in this line of work, that the only thing worse than losing your own pet is losing *someone else's* pet. The guilt is unbearable. I reminded Bob that he should keep searching in the area where my dogs lost the scent, then headed home.

An hour later, I walked in my front door to a ringing phone. It was Bob calling me from his veterinarian's office.

"You'll never believe it!" Bob exclaimed. "I found George!"

"Wonderful!" I answered. "Where was he?"

"Right after you left," Bob explained, "I got into my truck and decided to start searching along the orchard beyond where your dog lost the scent. I drove about a quarter mile down and made a right turn along the first side road I came to. I don't know what made me look, but I glanced to my left out into an open, plowed field. George was sitting out there in the middle of the field with his paw lifted in the air."

"Is he all right?"

"His left front leg is shattered," Bob said, "It looks like you were right about the skid marks—the vet thinks he was hit by a car. He was in shock and dehydrated, but he's alive." There was great relief in Bob's voice and I was happy for him. "He's going to need reconstructive surgery, but the vet says he ought to pull through like a champ."

"If it hadn't been for your dogs," Bob said before we hung up, "I wouldn't have known which direction to look."

I was thrilled. Rachel, as usual, had done her job with precision. Chase, thankfully, had proved herself as a valuable tracking tool. It felt great to work searches with happy endings—they made up for all of the sad ones. Although we didn't track right up to George, my search dogs established the correct direction of travel and helped Bob define and focus his search area. Still, a part of me wished I could have been there to actually witness happy reunions like when Andrea found Rocky and Bob found George. But, as it turned out, I didn't have to wait long. Thanks to a little terrier full of trouble, my wish was about to come true.

Chapter Fifteen
THE TROUBLE WITH TERRIERS

I had thought the article in the *Chronicle* garnered my pet detective work a lot of attention, but I hadn't seen anything yet. Before I knew it, I was answering calls from members of the media from all across the country who wanted to talk with me about my pet detective work. As I went with my dogs from case to case, I was confident in my ability to effectively and completely conduct a lost-pet search, but it was a huge adjustment to have people wanting to come along with notebooks, cameras, and long microphones with wooly slipcovers that my dogs innocently mistook for fuzzy toys. More than anything, I worried that the reporters would trivialize what I was doing, playing up the *Ace Ventura* angle at the expense of the serious nature of the searches.

But the producers who filmed us did a great job of capturing the true nature of our search work. One television program filmed Chase tracking a lost Chihuahua and Rachel finding a lost cat hiding in a back yard. We were filmed for two different shows on *Animal Planet*, both for lost cats that were found alive and well. And an appearance in *People* magazine resulted in interest from producers overseas who wanted to fly to California to film our searches.

One of the most surreal experiences in my pet detective career came when a producer from Canada called and asked to bring a film crew to record a few pet searches for a TV documentary. It was a show called *Dogs with Jobs* that would eventually air on PBS, Netflix, and the National Geographic channel. He flew down from Montreal and a soundman came in from San Francisco to spend six whole days tracking my movements with Rachel, A.J., Chase, and the volunteers who had been helping us on pet searches. To generate a number of searches in such a short time, the Humane Society of

Santa Clara Valley let me hang a poster at their lost-pet counter, offering free searches for missing pets during those six days.

The response was overwhelming. In less than a week, we conducted fifteen searches, with cameras in tow for all of them. Getting used to having a camera filming me while I interviewed the pet owners and set up the game plans for each search with the volunteers was awkward, but I was hopeful that the producer was spending enough time with us to realize that the nature of our work involved more than just working a search dog. I was encouraged that he took the time to film a long sit-down interview with me.

In the end, those interviews were interspersed throughout the footage of our searches, but it wasn't me who held viewer's attention. It wasn't even my ever camera-ready Rachel. The dog who stole the show was Bubba—a twenty-pound Jack Russell terrier with a personality that was larger than life.

Bubba's owner saw our sign at the animal shelter while he was looking for his lost dog. Jack Russells are well known for their high energy and intelligence, and many have personalities that seem more like Curious George than they do like any dog breed. They're highly trainable if you spend enough time working with them, but if you don't challenge their busy bodies and minds with some kind of activity, it doesn't take them long to find ways to amuse themselves.

Bubba got bored one afternoon and managed to work the back gate of his yard open just enough to squeeze himself through to freedom. He had about 20 minutes of head start on his owner, Omar Boswell, and that was enough to get him out of shouting range.

Omar knew that Jack Russells are a popular breed, and since Bubba was a good-looking, healthy little guy at that, there was a good chance someone would find his dog and decide to keep him. On the off chance that someone might take Bubba to the shelter, though, Omar headed there first, to make sure the staff knew he was looking for his dog. A dog like Bubba would have had a long line of people waiting to adopt him by the end of his seventy-two-hour waiting period.

When Omar saw my poster, he immediately called.

"This is a great dog," he said after he told me about the escape. "He's like my son. I've offered a large reward, but I haven't heard from anyone yet, and I have to get him back."

I responded to the call with A.J., Rachel, and Patti Kirby, one of my pet detective volunteers. Patti was new to our team and was the owner of Cleo, the missing cat whose case we solved using a DNA test. Like several of my other volunteers, Patti was so impressed with the concept of lost-pet services that once she had moved past her grief, she volunteered to respond as a dog handler whenever I needed her. This was Patti's first search and her first time handling either of my dogs. Patti and I turned up at Omar's home in San Jose, decked out in our florescent orange LOST PET RESCUE search vests, closely followed by our Canadian television producer with his fancy camera and the soundman with the fuzzy dog-toy-on-a-stick. I'm sure Omar wondered what he had gotten himself into.

Trying to work normally in spite of the camera, I scented A.J. on Bubba's bedding and proudly stood back and watched while my dog did his thing. A.J. started at the back gate, and it was immediately obvious that he was on the scent. He trotted down the side of the road, turning at some intersections and blowing straight through others, as if the little dog were right in front of him. We trailed three blocks, and then A.J. suddenly stopped, made a quick sniff-check of the circumference, and turned around and looked me in the eye.

The trail was dead.

I trusted A.J. enough to know that he wouldn't just halt on a trail like that unless it abruptly ended where he had stopped. And if that was the case, then chances were, just as Omar feared, someone in a car had probably stopped there, picked Bubba up, and continued on. It was the only explanation for the trail that suddenly went cold by the roadside, and it was the one that Omar had worried about from the minute Bubba turned up missing.

Thinking that maybe he had just missed a turn, I led A.J. back to the place that he had last had the scent. Sure enough, he picked up the scent trail and worked east, in a new direction for about one block.

What happened next was almost too strange a coincidence for me to believe. While I was jogging behind Patti and A.J., a passing SUV pulled over to the side of the street next to the producer who was focused on filming us. Easing the passenger window down, the driver leaned over to take a closer look at our strange posse.

"Excuse me," the young woman yelled to the producer, "but what are you looking for?"

Omar was the first one to the window. "I lost my dog. He's a four-year-old Jack Russell terrier named Bubba."

"I have your dog," the woman replied, with a hint of noticeable regret. "He's at my house right now."

What followed was an odd chaos created by the combination of Omar's elation that his dog would be coming home, the driver of the SUV's disappointment that she would not get to keep Bubba, and my producer's hasty hatching of a plan to get the happy-ending footage he wanted after working with me for the past six days.

Personally, I was thrilled that Omar was going to get his dog back. A.J. had worked a good scent trail and moved us in the right direction, and now, as far as I was concerned, my work was done.

But after some convincing, I agreed to take A.J. the remaining distance to this woman's house, to let him make an identification of Bubba for the cameras.

To his credit, A.J. did his job to a T when we got to the address, about a half mile away. I gave him a cheerful "Get to work!" when we arrived, and he did not walk, but lunged, toward the door of the house where Bubba was being sheltered.

The lady from the SUV, who was inside the house with Bubba, then opened the front door with Bubba snuggled in her arms. "He's such a cute dog," she said, as she gave Bubba one last peck on the top of his head. "I'm going to miss him."

Per the instructions of the producer, the woman then set Bubba down on the ground. The producer wanted to capture the actual reunion on film. In typical Jack Russell fashion, Bubba shot like a bullet the moment his terrier toes touched the ground, and as fast as his feet could carry him, he bolted the short distance to Omar and jumped up into his arms.

"Bubba!" Omar yelled. The tiny dog was licking Omar's face as he suspended Bubba in the air above him, both of them ecstatic to be together again.

And then Omar delighted everyone with one last surprise. "You know, we're raising a litter of Bubba's puppies at my house. If you like, since you took such good care of him, you can come and choose a puppy."

Suddenly everyone in our group was equally excited about our find: Bubba was licking Omar's face as if he'd missed him every minute, Omar was grinning from ear to ear, the woman who had hoped to have her very own Jack Russell was about to get a puppy, the camera crew had their happy reunion, Patti had worked A.J. on a successful case, and I was proud that my dog had "got his man." After all the disappointing endings to my searches, we'd finally found one suitable for a storybook.

Chapter Sixteen
END OF THE ROAD

On the heels of finding Bubba, something happened for me that I had all but given up on: I found a man. For years, I had longed for a marriage with a loving, supportive Christian husband, preferably one who would not balk at the inevitable dog slobber or mind Rachel's early-morning antics. At the very least, I wanted someone who supported my work and who wouldn't complain when a dog finagled its way up onto the bed.

Instead, I fell head over heels for David, a former police officer who was enamored of both me and my bloodhounds. I dove into the relationship pretty blindly because I was so eager for it to end up at the altar, followed by happily ever after. Four months, one sparkling ring from David, a hastily bought wedding gown, and an unexpected canine illness later, it became clear that I had made a mistake. The wedge that ultimately divided us came down to the one thing in my life that I was not willing to give up or negotiate about to ensure the happy marriage I'd been pining for. It came down to Rachel.

A few months before my scheduled wedding date, Rachel was diagnosed with a heart arrhythmia. I immediately cleared my schedule to make way for her appointments, raced her to a specialist, and spent a large hunk of money on veterinary treatment, including pricey heart pills.

To my surprise, David did not approve. He sat me down and explained that he had managed the health of his former dog by establishing what he called a "lifetime veterinary budget" when the dog was just a puppy. He had set aside six hundred dollars for the entire life of his terrier. The kicker was that his dog had managed to live, within that budget, to the ripe old age of fifteen. My fiancé looked me in the eyes and told me I needed to set a budget for Rachel's health care. I was appalled. I looked back at him and felt like I'd never seen him before. I was terrified that I was going to lose my beautiful, wonderful, devoted dog, and David's unrealistic budget only exacerbated my fears.

I decided then and there that there would be no "budget" for my dog's veterinary care. I would spend my last dime on her if I had to, and I was pretty sure I'd rack up credit card debt after that if there was a chance it would help. I couldn't believe that anyone—especially the man I loved—would ask me to look the other way while my dog suffered. A month later, after differences in our spiritual belief systems surfaced, our relationship completely unraveled. I gave David his ring back and moved forward with my life.

The months after my engagement fell apart, as what would have been our wedding date came and went, were a very lonely time for me. With Rachel, A.J., Chase, Myron and Yogi all sharing every square inch of my life, though, I was never really alone. My mom, my siblings, and my good friends, especially Jeanne and Becky, all took great pains to look out for me. There was a steady stream of phone calls, invitations to lunches, dinners, and movies as they all pitched in to try to fill the sudden, dramatic void in my social calendar.

Unfortunately, the National Center for Missing Pets, the nonprofit organization I had dreamed would come together and develop lost-pet services across the country, was by this time so deeply mired in paperwork and confusion that I doubted it would ever reach fruition. I had been blessed with a board and volunteers who would go to the ends of the earth to help find lost pets, but there was no one among us who knew how to navigate the convoluted process that was required to become a nonprofit in the first place. Sadly, when mistakes were made and our first application was rejected by the IRS, the whole organization went down the drain because no one knew for sure what to do next.

Then I faced yet another setback: a financial roadblock. The limp that had sidelined A.J. from search work was diagnosed as hip dysplasia. My trusty hound was in extreme pain and would need costly total-hip-replacement surgery. My savings had been drained building the nonprofit and paying for Rachel's expensive medical bills, but I wasn't about to sit by and watch while A.J. suffered. I put A.J. through the surgery and charged it to a credit card.

For the first time in nine years, I looked into resuming work as a police dispatcher. It was a job I hated, but it was something I knew, and it would pay my bills. The itty-bitty part of me that was a hard-core realist was starting to make a convincing argument that the pet detective gig might be a bust. I accepted a part-time job as a 9-1-1 dispatcher for the county of Santa Cruz.

After just two weeks on the job, I realized that I'd made a big mistake. It came to light the evening I answered a 9-1-1 call of someone reporting a forest fire burning by my cabin.

"9-1-1, what are you reporting?" I asked as another dispatcher assigned to train me listened in on the call.

"A fire," the young boy said. I felt my face drain when I noticed the address where the caller was dialing from. It was on the same block where I lived. My entire animal family was locked inside my tinder-dry cabin. Suddenly, horror stories of other dispatchers, police officers, and fire fighters having to handle emergency calls that involved witnessing the death of their own loved ones flooded my mind. I typed in what I thought was the correct code to initiate the fire department dispatch system, but it was the wrong code. My keyboard locked up.

"Do you see smoke or flames?" I asked, shaking. A simple report of smoke would require a fire official or even a deputy to check the area to determine whether a brigade of fire trucks was needed, whereas a report of flames would require the immediate dispatch of fire trucks.

"Flames," he said. I felt my face go pale, my computer still locked up. I tapped, then frantically pounded on the stupid keyboard, but could not generate the computer "call" to activate the fire department. Suddenly, I couldn't breathe. All I could think about was how I was sitting helplessly inside a dispatch dungeon while my family—A.J., Chase, Rachel, Myron, and Yogi—were all trapped inside my cabin, located right where this fire was reportedly blazing away.

All of my police training, including my training as a police detective, had taught me to ask open-ended questions. An open-ended question in this case would've been to instruct the caller, "Tell me what you see." But because I was catatonic with fear, I asked closed-ended questions. I immediately assumed the worst: that my three dogs and my two cats were all trapped alive inside my burning cabin while I sat far away working at a job I hated, unable to save their lives.

"Do you see any cabins on fire?" I asked, assuming he did because in my worst nightmare (which I was living at that moment) *I* certainly saw my cabin on fire.

"Yes," was all he said.

By now, I realized something was wrong about this call. No other calls of a fire were coming in, and this boy seemed awfully calm, certainly calmer than I was. There were no background noises, and he did not elaborate on any of his close-ended answers.

"Let me talk to your parents," I said. The brat hung up the phone.

"It's just a crank call," my trainer said, trying to put me at ease. But I was so rattled, I couldn't see straight. A deputy was dispatched to the phone booth the kid had called from and, of course, there was nothing wrong there. No child, no fire, no problem.

That night, I showered the dogs with extra treats and cuddled with Myron in my lap. Even though finances were tight and I wasn't sure how I was going to pay my bills, I was no longer willing to work at a job I resented or where I felt that helpless again. The following day, I resigned from the dispatch job.

Thankfully, a month later an opportunity came along that seemed like the chance I had been waiting for: a real job, searching for lost pets, with one of the biggest humane organizations in the United States. I was offered a position with the American Humane Association (AHA).

This opportunity came as the result of my aggressively cold calling some of the nation's larger animal nonprofit organizations. I got nowhere until I called AHA, where I was able to bend the ear of the director of animal protection, Nicholas "Nick" Gilman. Nick totally supported my vision to develop lost-pet services. However, he could not simply hire me from scratch to develop the program idea that I had in mind. He could, however, consider me for a position that he felt would be an ideal match. He suggested that I apply for a management position for AHA's Emergency Animal Relief program.

The job was a compromise on my vision for lost-pet services. I would be using my dogs to search for pets lost in manmade and natural disasters, not missing pets who escaped through an open door or a hole in the fence. I struggled with the decision to take this job because there were already several organizations working to help save pets in disasters, but no program or organization was working to help families experiencing the everyday "disaster" of when their pet went missing. However, I concluded that working to find lost pets in any capacity was better than doing nothing at all.

The fly in the ointment was that the job was in Los Angeles, and if I wanted it, I'd have to move immediately. My affection for Santa Cruz had never wavered since my first trip chugging over the mountains pulling my belongings in a U-Haul, but I was willing to gamble again on what seemed like the career opportunity of a lifetime. I rented a big four-bedroom house in Simi Valley, once again packed up everything I owned, and headed to Southern California. It was the summer of 2000, and it seemed fitting that this new career move should be tied to a new century.

I still remember the day I crossed over the "Grapevine," the twisty pass that divided my old stomping grounds, the central San Joaquin Valley, from the massive expanse of Los Angeles. As was typical of Southern California in the heat of summer, there had been a wildfire and choking smoke had smothered the San Fernando Valley. The sky was mucky brown so I was forced to drive with my headlights on to navigate through the smog. I pulled off the freeway into a shopping center and cried. I couldn't believe that I had left the beauty of Santa Cruz to live in a smoggy, urban desert. But I settled into my new home, took in a housemate, and began to recruit a core group of twenty volunteers who wanted to learn how to train dogs to locate lost pets.

Through the local paper, I put the word out that we were looking for volunteers who wanted to assist in lost-pet rescue work. I developed a system for evaluating potential search dogs and exposed the rookie dogs to strange sights, sounds, and sensations to see which dogs were gutsy. I clanged pots together, banged a broom around in close proximity to the dog, and clambered around on crutches that I then raised high above my head in a semi-threatening manner. I only moved forward with the dogs that proved they were not aggressive toward or fearful of humans, dogs, or cats.

Once I determined a dog had the right temperament, then I tested it to see if it had the right drive to make it as a search dog. I exposed the dogs to the scent of a crated target cat (Myron) and watched their reaction. The dogs that wiggled with excitement but were not aggressive towards kitties became the cat-detection dogs. The dogs that went crazy with excitement when someone ran around the corner with another dog became the trailing dogs. We started a weekly training session where I worked with each dog and handler on beginning-search problems. I had plans to develop a classroom certification program, but training the humans would have to wait—my priority was to train and certify the dogs first.

In my "spare" time, I occasionally had a chance to work my own dogs on searches for missing pets. Mercifully, Rachel's health seemed to have improved. With medication, her heart arrhythmia stabilized, and she was as eager to work as ever. Our veterinarian in Santa Cruz, Charlie Miller, even nominated Rachel for an award: The California Veterinary Medical Association's Animal Hall of Fame award given every year to any domesticated species that demonstrates "unselfish and courageous accomplishments." Dr. Miller was proud of Rachel's pet-finding successes and felt that her extraordinary achievements deserved recognition.

But the honor, much to my chagrin, went to a three-legged therapy cat and not to Rachel. "This kitty had an important job, too," I consoled Rachel, as if she might be embittered by the loss.

But Rachel was as happy as ever. Nothing pleased her more than to put on her search vest and follow a scent for me, so I always gave her first crack at a new search, as much for her as for the lost pets we were seeking. When we had a dry spell between searches, I'd stick Yogi or Myron in a crate to give Rachel a chance to use her skills. She was like a kid at the playground on every search—giddy and excited and determined to get every minute of pleasure out of her job. It always made me smile to see my elderly dame of a Weimaraner reduced to skipping and prancing around like a year-old puppy at the prospect of finding a cat.

In the late fall of 2000, though, something changed in Rachel. At first, I couldn't put my finger on it. She looked a little different and suddenly had a solemn, strained expression on her face. But soon, the slight change turned into something much bigger. The jowl at the corner of her mouth drooped slightly on the left side. I noticed that she wasn't hearing well. And then she began to stumble a bit when she walked. In just a matter of days, Rachel was turning her head to the right to see or hear me, and striking out awkwardly with her left paw when she walked.

The veterinarian explained that there must be a neurological cause for the virtual shutdown of Rachel's left side. She was blind in her left eye, deaf in her left ear, and could not smell from her left nostril. The vet ordered a MRI. It was New Year's Eve when I drove the two hours to the clinic in Orange County that performed the testing. The news after the test was devastating. Rachel had a large, malignant brain tumor.

I had three choices for Rachel's care. I could pursue radiation and chemotherapy for her, but the vet told me bluntly that Rachel was not going to get better with any treatment. It might buy her four to six months, but that was the best we could hope for. I could medicate her and wait for her life to end in its own time. Or I could have my beloved dog euthanized.

For the first twenty-four hours, I huddled at home with my dogs and didn't talk with anyone. I didn't know what to say, and I didn't want any unsolicited advice.

That night when I took her out back for the final potty break of the day, Rachel alerted. It was warm and very windy and even with her awkward gait and her quickly failing coordination and senses, there was no mistaking her signals that Rachel had something to show me. Her nose twitched. Her tail wiggled. Her head turned, alert as she sought to pinpoint the source of the odor that had caught the attention of her half-operational nose. And then she hurried over to me and did her best to jump up on me.

"What did you find?" I asked in disbelief. "Show me." I followed as she half-stumbled, half-pulled me over to the base of a giant, brushy tree in the backyard of my house. Rachel was shaking from head to toe, in part from her excitement, and in part from the effort she had put forth to give the alert, but she was determined to show me something. I looked up but couldn't see a thing and for a second, I doubted my dog. But Rachel insisted she had something to give me, so I left her there to get a flashlight, a little afraid to leave her alone. I returned with the light and cast the beam up into the tree.

There, crouched high in the branches, was a longhaired, black cat that I had never seen before. The poor kitty was a little panicked to be the focus of such unwelcome canine and human attention.

"Good girl," I said, without the exuberant praise that my dog deserved for her find. I choked back tears as I switched off the flashlight, knelt down, and hugged Rachel. "Let's go inside and get you some cheese."

The following morning, I decided to call Becky, who now lived hundreds of miles away where she still worked as the office manager in Dr. Miller's office. Becky had seen dogs with every health problem there is, and she loved Rachel. I knew her advice would be informed by both affection and knowledge—the best I could ask for. I asked Becky to tell me what she thought was the best thing for me to do—treatment or euthanasia.

"Kat, there is no 'best' choice," she explained. "If you take her through treatment, it will be difficult, and if you put her to sleep it will be difficult. This is *cancer*—there's no cure. There is no right decision for you to make, but whatever you decide, I will be there for you." Becky shocked me by telling me that she had a few days off from work and she wanted to fly down and see me. My dear friend, who didn't have a dime to spare at the time, called back with her flight information for when she would arrive the following morning at the airport.

That night, when I checked my e-mail, there was a message forwarded from a friend, a cancer survivor, from a woman who had undergone a nontraditional treatment for a brain tumor. In the letter, the woman talked about what she described as the "excruciating, vise grip-like pain" in her head, and suddenly, I knew what the change had been in Rachel's countenance weeks before. I realized that the slight alteration in her beautiful face was because she had been in pain.

I turned off the computer and crawled into my bed, where Rachel was curled and lightly sleeping on the second pillow. I couldn't believe that I was going to lose her, but from that moment on I knew that I would not make her suffer just so I could share her companionship, either.

The next day, when I picked Becky up at the Burbank Airport, I told her I had decided to have Rachel put to sleep. It was a great comfort to have Becky with me. When we arrived back at my house, I called the veterinarian and made an appointment for late in the afternoon. I knew that if I didn't follow through on my decision to end Rachel's suffering soon, I would lose my determination to do it at all. I set about spending the remainder of the day trying to make Rachel happy.

I took a surprisingly willing Yogi and popped her into her crate, then "hid" her next to a rose bush in my yard so Rachel could find her. When Rachel saw me bring out her search vest, she struggled to her feet and eagerly waited to have it put on. "Where's the kitty?" I asked, and gave her Yogi's brush to sniff.

Rachel was eager and excited to be looking for her favorite cat. You could hardly call it a "search," really, because Rachel could actually see the crate in front of her and she began to strain to go up to it. I felt a little embarrassed that I had made this find so easy for her but I didn't want to cause her exhaustion by making her work to find Yogi. She only had to walk ten yards before she was happily nuzzling Yogi's cage, drained but pleased with herself, and looking for her piece of cheese.

Becky and I spent the next hour talking about Rachel's adventures and her amazing altruism toward other animals. Rachel stretched out on the couch between us as we took turns stroking her silky ears, rubbing her tummy, and feeding her tiny globs of Brie. I kept checking the clock on the wall, as it ticked away the minutes I had left with my dog.

Rachel wasn't able to jump up in the truck on her own. Her legs and her uncoordinated balance wouldn't let her do it. Becky and I picked her up between us and gently helped her into her crate. While Becky waited in the truck with Rachel, I went back inside and picked up the bag I had packed for my dog's last trip. It contained her orange search vest, a pair of my dirty white socks, and a plastic bag of cheese. With my stomach in knots and tears streaming down my face, I climbed into the driver's seat.

At the veterinarian's office, Becky mercifully took over. She requested that Rachel be given a mild sedative first, so she would be relaxed and not fearful in the office. We were taken to an exam room where we laid out a blanket and sat on the ground next to my dog, Becky on one side, me on the other. Rachel's eyes lit up when she saw her search vest, but she slumped against me as I put it on her. The vest was symbolic, of course, but I wanted Rachel to leave my life the same way she had come into it—a heroic search dog.

In the beginning, her heroism had all been in my imagination—all the things we were going to do together. She was going to be the search dog that changed my life. In our years together, my expectations of Rachel had shifted time and again, and she had never let me down. She'd been an ideal search dog when she was working criminal investigations. She'd been the perfect pet when I kept her out of the field for almost four years, greeting me happily at the end of each day and snoring on my bed each night, as though there was nothing she'd rather do than hang out at home while the bloodhounds got to go to work. And when it was time for Rachel to work again, when she was called back into action to search for lost pets, she had been more heroic and steadfast than I could have ever asked.

I looked at her now, sick and weak, but still thumping her tail as she rested her head on my lap, and I was overwhelmed by my feelings. I felt both grief that I was about to lose her and gratitude that I had been so blessed by God to have her in my life for the past eleven years.

Once the vest was on, I offered Rachel the cheese. She took a small nibble, but as had been the case in recent weeks, she didn't want much. The veterinarian came in, prepared to give Rachel the first injection. Within a few minutes after it was administered, I could see her slowly begin to relax. She nuzzled the socks between her front paws and gave a deep sigh. The strain that had become ever present on her face started to let up as she drifted out of consciousness. As the second and final injection was given, I cupped Rachel's face in my palms and rested my cheek against hers. "You're such a good girl. I don't know what I'm going to do without you, Rachel."

And in a matter of minutes, the faithful dog who had been my friend and companion, who had dramatically changed my life and made me believe that I could accomplish anything, was gone.

CHAPTER SEVENTEEN

NEW TRAILS AND TALES

I was still reeling from losing Rachel when I was blindsided by a different kind of bad news. Due to budget cuts at American Humane Association, my job was being eliminated. I had no idea where to go next with my life.

After weighing all the options, I decided to go back to Fresno. My mother had early Alzheimer's disease. It was clear it was no longer safe for her to live alone, thus the obvious solution was for me to take care of her. When you're forty, unemployed, and you move back home to live with your mother, people talk, but I felt good about my decision to spend time with my family and regroup.

I knew that a few of my friends didn't approve of my decision. They probably thought I was sitting around the house in my jammies all day eating bon-bons. Though I admit I *did* indulge in the pajama thing from time to time, for the most part I threw myself into laying the foundation for a new national nonprofit organization. Despite the failure of the first attempt, I still believed it could, and should, be done.

Two weeks after I got home, my sweet cat Yogi suddenly collapsed and stopped breathing. I administered Pet CPR and rushed her to my vet but she did not survive. I was reminded again of the sky-high emotional stakes I had in my pets. I struggled to keep myself above the invisible line of depression.

Two months later, I traveled to Washington, D.C., to speak at the American Humane Association's annual conference. It was September 11, 2001, and I was in a Marriott Hotel just three blocks from where Flight 77 crashed into the Pentagon. It took six days, including a hairy drive in a rental car from D.C. to Denver, through near-tornado weather in Kansas, and a choppy ride in a tiny prop plane, before I landed safely in Fresno.

I was a wreck.

I sat in front of my TV for weeks and watched the nation change. People donated to disaster organizations but donations for animal organizations plummeted. The economy took a nosedive. Suddenly, the issue of lost pets seemed like an unimportant cause. For the first time in years, I didn't want to pioneer lost-pet services. I felt exhausted, as if all the effort and all the years of trying to make my pet-rescue hobby into a career and a national cause were hitting me at once. I felt like I didn't want to do it anymore.

But thank God, a woman named Pat Singleton and her lost cat, Zachary, created the turnaround I needed. It was two weeks before Christmas 2001 and I happened to glance at the classified ads. I noticed an ad that read: "REWARD: Lost Siamese cat, declawed. Sunnyside & Shaw in Clovis." I had looked at many lost-pet classifieds before, but this one caught my eye for two reasons: First, the location was just around the corner from my home, and second, I surmised that a declawed Siamese was likely an indoor-only cat that had escaped outdoors and it was most probably hiding nearby. I decided to call the owner and advise him or her to use a humane trap as a recovery tool.

Pat was eighty-four and lived in a senior center. She began to cry when I said I could tell her how to find Zachary. I asked her if she had conducted an aggressive search outdoors, and she had not. It turned out she was disabled with rheumatoid arthritis. Her hands were curled, stiff and nearly useless. She couldn't even make lost-cat posters, let alone get out and search the grounds. She told me that Zachary had bolted out the door when the facility's housecleaner turned on the vacuum. When Pat told me that Zachary often hid under the bed, even from Pat, I knew he was likely close by and hidden. If Pat did not recover Zachary, he would most likely become absorbed into the feral cat population. He would likely suffer from emaciation and dehydration, and as a lifetime indoor cat, he would probably not survive long on his own.

"You need to rent a humane trap," I told Pat. Even though I lived just a few blocks away, I didn't have the energy, or desire, to try and trap the cat myself. I was hoping that a member of Pat's family or a friend would help her set up a trap. But no one did. The following day, I called Pat again to see if she had had any luck. She was even more distraught and she still had not rented a trap.

She needed me to do it.

"Can't you please come help me?" Pat asked.

At that time I didn't have a humane trap, I didn't have Rachel, and I didn't have any of the fancy, expensive equipment that I had used before. The infrared camera had been borrowed through my police contacts from a company in the San Francisco Bay Area that I had lost contact with; the search camera was also on loan and had been returned; and my amplified listening device and cat traps were boxed away in storage in Simi Valley, along with almost all my other belongings. All these tools suddenly seemed a million miles away from Fresno.

I only had my knowledge of how and where to look for a lost cat. Still, Pat had shamed me into it. I got up, got dressed, and drove to the senior center. She gave me a hero's welcome, and I searched around the apartments, where there were very few hiding places. I never saw or heard Zachary, but my gut and my experience told me he was still close by, hiding in fear. Pat was disappointed, but the next day when I spoke with her again, she was beyond that. She was depressed, and ready to give up hope. It had been nine days since Zachary had vanished, and Pat knew the chances of his safe return were dwindling.

"I just think someone took him into their home," Pat said as she cried over the phone. "I've accepted that I'll never see him again." Pat was experiencing "grief avoidance," a behavior that causes pet owners to stop searching for a lost pet because they want to stop grieving. But I knew better. With his skittish temperament, Zachary was certainly *not* sitting inside someone's house, curled in a ball on a warm lap. He was hiding in silence within earshot of Pat's apartment.

Having no cash, but armed with an overused credit card, I went to a local hardware store and bought a humane trap. I justified the purchase by deciding it was a Christmas present to myself. I was ready to find this woman's cat, even if it was the last pet detective case I ever worked. And at the time, I figured it probably would be.

I called Pat that afternoon and told her I'd be coming over that night to set a trap for Zachary. A few hours later, the phone rang.

"This is Pat's daughter," the unfamiliar voice on the line said, "Mom wanted me to call and tell you that Zachary is home!"

The humane trap wasn't needed after all. Zachary was hiding in a woodpile just a hundred feet from Pat's front door. I had searched around that pile of wood but never saw or heard Zachary. Pat's daughter said that she, too, had searched the woodpile more than once, calling her mother's cat at the top of her lungs. Zachary had been there the entire time, but had remained silent. He eventually reached a threshold, though, where he was thirsty and hungry enough to meow a response.

Pat was grateful I'd insisted she hold out hope, and I was glad I'd met someone who made me pick up where I had left off. I was ready to pick up the pieces of my shattered pipe dream and move forward. My soul knew that God had a purpose and a plan for my life and I sensed that my work as a pet detective was not over. Cautiously, I recruited a small board of directors and, once again, started my quest to build a national nonprofit organization that could develop community-based lost-pet services.

We called the organization Missing Pet Partnership. We decided we would develop partnerships with animal shelters, rescue groups, and other organizations and that our focus would be to provide training. Because the training of the search dogs was the most technically difficult piece of the pie, our vision was to ultimately build a training facility where we could house, train, and certify pet detective search dogs. Once the dogs were trained and ready to search for lost pets, we planned to issue them to lost-pet recovery teams and provide the necessary classroom training for the volunteers. It took us over a year, but our board of directors finally submitted our application for nonprofit status to the IRS. In spite of my previous failure with the first nonprofit, I was willing to try again.

In the meantime, the house seemed just a little too quiet without Rachel and Yogi. I was finally ready to hear the pitter-patter of new paws in my life. So I opened my house, and my heart, to three new family members; Cheeto, Sadie, and Kody.

I didn't intentionally go out and get another cat to replace Yogi. She was one of a kind, and it would have been pointless to try. I just missed the presence of an orange cat in my life. Once again, I found myself at the local animal shelter, this time adopting an active, cheddar cheese-colored kitten that tugged at my heartstrings. I named him Cheeto.

As he grew older, Cheeto would stalk and pounce on poor Myron, insist on squeezing into the "no cats allowed" dog areas because he would only drink slobbery dog water (saving the cat water bowl for tipping over), scale and destroy my cloth curtains, and dangle precariously from the mini-blinds. Once he discovered that he could make me yell, there was no stopping his antics. Cheeto was a unique combination of obnoxious and charming, and that was never more evident than the morning he crawled into my closet and sharpened his talons on the front of my unused wedding dress. I didn't know whether to kiss him or kill him, but after the initial shock, I loved him all the more for desecrating my most painful reminder of my broken engagement.

In spite of his exasperating behavior, Cheeto had more character than any feline I had ever seen. I trained him to sit on his haunches and wave for a dab of liverwurst or a piece of dried salmon. Because he loved dogs, Cheeto was easy to train as a target cat and excelled in his job. He was fearless, loved attention from people, and would ham it up. He acted more like a dog than a cat and was adored by everyone, both human and canine, he encountered.

After Cheeto came Sadie. She was a four-year-old female Weimaraner donated to me by a family in Fresno after they heard about the search work I had done with Rachel. Sadie's color was "blue," a dark gray with a bluish tint. In addition to the color difference, Sadie had other features that were very different from Rachel—she was stubborn to the core!

As an "alpha dog" Sadie had a refuse-to-obey-the-owner streak that took me by surprise. If she was just about to lie down and I gave the "down" command, she would freeze in defiance and refuse to budge. If something was not *her* idea, then it wasn't a good idea at all. She had a bad and unlawful habit of breaking and entering the cat's-only dining area to rob Cheeto and Myron of their dinner. She also had a low tolerance for noise and panicked to the point of shivering uncontrollably at the sound of vacuum cleaners, lawn mowers, gunshots, thunder, and fireworks. Because of her fearful nature, Sadie was not a dog that I could travel with like I had traveled with Rachel. A plane ride would probably petrify her. She was also a snapper in that if you tried to move her when she did not want to move, she'd bite you.

But Sadie's Weimaranerness helped ease a little of the pain I still felt—that I guess I'll always feel—about losing Rachel. Sadie was a dog I grew to love, and she did extremely well in her training. Like Rachel, Sadie absolutely loved kitties, and she was easy to read when she picked up cat scent. Not only would her tail wiggle but she'd let out a series of whining noises. I knew that someday, Sadie would find many lost cats.

Two years after my return to Fresno, after a promising start, Missing Pet Partnership floundered. The IRS dragged its governmental feet and months ticked away without any significant development with the organization. Missing Pet Partnership existed as a nonprofit on paper, but in reality, we were still just a passionate cause, one that had cost me five years of personal and financial sacrifices. Our Web site gave the appearance that we were a full-fledged organization, but in fact I played the rolls of executive director, director of training, receptionist, Web site developer, marketing director, director of development, volunteer coordinator, and lost-pet consultant. The phone for our organization rang into the back bedroom of my mother's home.

I decided that I wasn't willing to wait for the organization—it would have to catch up to me. I recruited and began to train a new group of local volunteers and dogs. I fine-tuned my techniques for evaluating search dogs and came up with a great mix of rookie dogs. I called them the "Fresno Fifteen" because I quickly discovered that I could only train fifteen dogs and volunteers at a time. I even managed to rescue two dogs from the local shelter and found volunteers willing to foster and train them.

One of these dogs, Suzie, was a hyper and destructive Jack Russell terrier that loved cats. Suzie was a dog that I initially intended to place in another city with a partnering shelter. But Suzie's "foster father," Hardin Weaver, loved the little dog. The two were inseparable. It wasn't long before I realized I'd never be able to take Suzie from Hardin so we officially made their fostering relationship an adoption and "hired" Suzie to be Missing Pet Partnership's local cat-detection dog. Over time, Hardin became more than a volunteer to me—he was a father figure, camping buddy, and my best friend. Hardin turned out to be the primary encouragement and sounding board for me during my years in Fresno. He encouraged me to stick with developing Missing Pet Partnership and to follow my dream of crafting a teen pet detective mystery novel that ultimately took several years for me to finish.

I fell in love with my group of Fresno volunteers and their dogs, and we all looked forward to our Saturday morning and Thursday evening training sessions. Just like the volunteers I had trained in Half Moon Bay, Santa Cruz, and Simi Valley, the Fresno Fifteen turned into a dedicated and passionate group. In addition to training their search dogs, I put these volunteers through the first-ever Missing Animal Response pet detective training course. Their training included instruction in lost-pet behavior, high-tech equipment certification, search dog applications, the collection and analysis of physical evidence, and search probability theory.

During one training session a final joy was added to my life, the one that most helped to restore me. A woman brought a mixed breed mutt that she wanted to either donate to our program or take to the pound. It was a wild little forty-pound, yellowish-gold, whippet mix with sweet brown eyes, a black mask, and triangle-shaped ears. Her color and facial features reminded me of Disney's Old Yeller with a pointy needle-nose. Kody had an exuberant love for people, other dogs, and cats. Even though she jumped up on people and was hard to settle down, Kody's charm immediately earned her a chance to go home with one of our volunteers.

But after one week of digging and chewing her way into that volunteer's life, Kody ended up at *my* house. This was supposed to be a temporary arrangement until I found another volunteer who could foster her, but in a matter of only a couple hours, I'd decided to keep her for myself. I fell in love with how incredibly smart, capable, and motivated the energetic little dog was, and I accepted her, digging, chewing, jumping up, and all.

Kody played harder than any dog I had ever seen. Every evening she transformed my back yard into a made-for-whippet racetrack and transitioned from Kody-the-search-dog to Old Yeller-on-methamphetamine. Kody's hyperkinetic energy was contagious, and I loved having all the excitement of this larger-than-life dog around me. It shocked me how quickly I had fallen for her, but when I thought about it, everything about Kody felt good and familiar. Kody loved to have her chest scratched, just like A.J. She was fascinated with foreign scents and when in our back yard her nose was glued to the ground, just like Chase. And through her superior motivation and willingness to do anything for a piece of cheese, I found a little bit of Rachel inside this once-unwanted mutt.

Chase adopted Kody as her long-lost buddy. For the first time in years I saw Chase romp and play with another dog. And all the new life in my house managed to liven up even stalwart A.J. He didn't actually get out and run laps with Chase and Kody, his searching days long since past, but their frenzied playing caught his attention, and he suddenly decided that it was important to him that they see he was the elder statesman of the house. He made sure that he was the first to receive the treats, the ear rubs, and the coveted scratch on the chest. I suspect that A.J. shared some of his secrets with Kody and Sadie, because not long after they joined my household, both dogs were ready for a real trail, and so was I.

The mist from the heavy December fog that smothered the San Joaquin Valley during the night had finally started to rise. Once again, I found myself standing in Fresno, ready to work my first search with a talented, critter-happy dog that loved cheese and lived to search. Although my circumstances were much different than when I first worked Rachel on the Fresno warehouse fire in 1990, I had come full circle.

I unloaded Kody from her crate and prepared her for work. It was 2002, two years since I had worked a search. But thankfully, Missing Pet Partnership had opened the doors for me to train and work search dogs once again. We were ready to go out into the community and offer the lost-pet services that I had been developing and pushing for nearly a decade.

I buckled Kody into her tracking harness, secured her bright orange "Search Dog" vest, and looked her over. This search was for Max, a missing cat, and it was going to be Kody's first. If search work with Kody and Sadie turned out to be anything like it had been with Rachel, I would remember the details of this moment for years to come. Kody looked up at me with her soft brown eyes, eager to get going. She'd had enough practice runs by now to know that putting on the orange vest meant another big chance to win praise and cheese. She couldn't wait.

At that moment, I realized how proud I was of my new dog. Sometime during our months of training, I had stopped looking at her and seeing the ways in which she was different from Rachel. I loved this little dog in her own right, and this day was a new beginning for both of us. And although Missing Pet Partnership was still lagging behind my pace, I had incredible passion and unshakable faith in my God-given pipe dream. I knew this new organization would succeed and that my efforts had not been in vain. But best of all, I had a little yellow dog with a big heart, willing to do whatever I asked her to do.

"Do you wanna work?" I asked. After months of training, Kody had already learned this command. She reared up on her hind legs, straining as I grasped her collar, her legs flailing in the air with excitement, her tail wagging in utter delight. Placing the gauze pad beneath her nose, I presented Kody with the scent of Max the missing cat. Her wet black nose wiggled as she inhaled the scent.

"Kody, take scent," I commanded. "Search!"

And with that, my dog and I surged forward, moving together into a promising new season as pioneering pet detectives.

EPILOGUE

It was a warm, breezy day in July 2008 when I found myself back in Santa Cruz. This was my first time back to the coastal town since I'd moved away eight years before. I was happy to be there to train a new group of pet detectives, yet sad about the other reason I was there: it was time to spread the ashes of my four Santa Cruz heroes.

Seven years prior to this, I had a terrible year when both Rachel and Yogi died. Then in 2004, I lost A.J. to kidney failure, just a few months after the publication of my first book. Four years later, in April 2008, shortly before I moved north to Seattle, I lost Chase to cancer. She was the last of my police dogs, and when she died, I felt my final connection with police work die with her.

The plans I had for that July day were too emotional to carry out alone. Needing support, I had invited two special friends to help me: Becky Hiatt, who had loved and cared for all three of my dogs, and Berry Minott, a producer friend who agreed to film the ash scattering for me.

Our first stop was in Scotts Valley on South Navarra Drive. This is where A.J. had his one and only felony walk-up-find: the case where he tracked down and identified the burglary suspect. It was my most memorable and enjoyable law enforcement search with A.J. and represented my passion for hunting criminals. I choked back my emotions as I spread the ashes of my friend A.J. along the last part of the suspect's trail, in the area where A.J. found the perpetrator hiding in the brush. The exact spot where the suspect had hidden was now inside a fenced yard, but I managed to spread A.J.'s ashes under a willow tree that I knew was there back when we worked the case in 1996.

Our next stop was at my old cabin in Felton where I planned to spread the ashes of my first target cat, Yogi. I wanted to spread her ashes in the ivy set under a grove of redwood trees next to my mailbox. This was the spot where my reluctant target cat spent countless hours napping. The nostalgia of the moment was lost to my concern that someone would catch me dumping an unknown powdery substance on private property. Even though it used to be *my* property, the current residents did not know me. They probably would not appreciate having dead cat ashes dumped into their front yard. But I didn't care—I flung Yogi's ashes in one swoop of the arm, jumped into the car, and Berry, Becky, and I sped off, in classic *Thelma and Louise* style.

The next stop was the hardest of the day. We drove to an area on the U.C. Santa Cruz campus that overlooked the massive Pogonip Park, the location of Rachel's cadaver search where she found the human jaw bone, a search that launched her career as a search dog. As I stood at the edge of the cliff and surveyed the forested park below, the wind suddenly kicked up. Tears streamed down my cheeks as I opened the plastic bag and threw Rachel's ashes high into the air. It was fitting for the ashes of an air scenting dog like Rachel to be carried away by the wind. It was difficult to let go of her, but I finally did.

The final stop of our adventure was in the town of Hollister on Fairview Road. My plan was to spread Chase's ashes along the route where she had tracked the scent of George, the missing Airedale. My emotions were raw because it had only been three months since Chase had been euthanized. She was a fierce tracker, and even though she had helped to recover several missing dogs, she always seemed to walk in the shadow of Rachel and A.J.'s work. Chase was loyal, she was goofy, and she was a blast to run behind. She had enriched my life and I had reserved a very special place in my heart for her—and for her ashes.

When we arrived at the address of the search, I noticed the mailbox still had the name "Pyle" on it. Bob Pyle had been in his seventies back when Chase tracked George's scent nine years before. Becky suggested we knock on the door, but I doubted Bob was still alive. And if he was, I didn't think he would remember me.

But Bob was very much alive and he certainly did remember me. When I explained the purpose of our visit—that we were there to spread Chase's ashes along Fairview Road when I noticed his name was still on the mailbox—Bob thanked me again for how Chase had helped save George's life. Bob explained that George had not only recovered from the surgery to repair his broken leg, he had also gone on to become a champion agility dog, a show dog, and even a therapy dog. The real shocker was when Bob asked, "Would you like to come inside and meet him?"

I was completely blown away to hear George was still alive! Bob led Berry, Becky and me into his house where I knelt down in front of the aging, fourteen-year-old Airedale, his tail thumping with delight. As I stroked his wire-like fur, I listened to Bob tell stories of the long, satisfying life he'd had with his dog, thanks to Chase. As I sat and listened to the stories, I couldn't have been more proud of Chase. I'd been given the blessing of meeting one of the many lost pets my talented search dogs had found. It was an incredible gift on this very special day of closure.

The sun set over the farmlands of Hollister as I walked along Fairview Road, spreading the ashes of Chase, my last police dog. We finished the evening with a sushi dinner and a toast to the memory of Rachel, A.J., Yogi, and Chase—four incredible animal souls that had forever changed my life and the lives of many people and their beloved pets.

Whenever I'm asked to share my "most memorable" search conducted with my search dogs, I fondly think about a particular missing-person case, not a pet detective case. It was a search that took place a year before my entry into pet detective work and taught me a critical lesson about a topic many people, myself included, grapple with; the willingness to trust.

A call had come in that my tracking dogs were needed in the search for a suicidal man who was armed with a gun. I holstered my pistol, grabbed my search pack, and led A.J. from the warmth of my cozy cabin out into the chilly night. Dropping the tailgate on my truck, I hoisted A.J. up into the wire transport cage designated for my four legged passengers.

"Do you wanna work?" I asked as I climbed into my truck and glanced in my rearview mirror. A.J. was standing in his crate. Although his sweet, Bambi-brown eyes were set inside droopy eyelids that conveyed the appearance of sadness, I wasn't fooled—A.J. loved to track. His plump tail thumped against the wires of his cage as he let out a single "Rooooooo," which I knew meant, "Yes!"

As I pulled away from my cabin, the beam from my headlights illuminated a path through the pitch-black darkness of winding mountain roads. This search was located in Paradise Park, a small, residential community of cabins nestled within the majestic redwoods. This particular area was often blanketed with a layer of cool, coastal fog. There was a matrix of small roads with clusters of cabins that made up the tight-knit community. I looked forward to searching in this area knowing that the shade from the redwoods combined with the moisture from the fog would hydrate the tiny scent particles, making it easy for A.J. to track the missing man.

By the time I pulled up to the Command Post, it was already 5:30 a.m. I noticed the usual mix of patrol cars, rescue vans, and volunteer search-and-rescue vehicles. My friend Jeanne Mason was also there with her golden retriever, Kea. Once we signed in, Jeanne and I were quickly given our assignments. Stacey, Jeanne's daughter, was assigned as my back-up person. While I worked A.J., Stacey would track our location with a map and operate the radio. Jason Dawson, another volunteer with the search-and-rescue team, would act as Jeanne's backup. We agreed that I would be the first to start searching with A.J. and that Jeanne would follow with Kea moments later.

Once at the missing man's cabin, I strapped the leather tracking harness on A.J. and attached a thirty-foot web lead. I felt a surge of adrenaline pulse through my veins. By this time, I knew I was doing the work God had created me to do—I was *born* to search! A.J. picked up on my excitement and began to prance with impatience. I led him over to the missing man's parked car, opened the driver's door, and allowed A.J. to sniff the high concentration of scent particles embedded in the fuzzy, faux sheep skin steering wheel cover.

"Search!" I commanded. A.J. immediately followed the man's scent trail as he checked an area behind the cabin. He quickly changed directions and then headed down a residential street away from the missing man's cabin.

Moments later, my radio crackled as Jeanne reported that Kea had also picked up a scent trail and was tracking in the same direction where A.J., Stacey, and I were moving. A.J. led us over a rickety wooden bridge and as we reached the pavement on the other side, I heard a noise behind me. It was Jeanne, Jason, and Kea and they were closing in fast. I decided to stop A.J. and allow Kea to work past us.

I hate to admit this, but I had more faith in Kea than I had in my own dog! A bloodhound handler must blindly run behind their dog and trust that the dog is following the scent of the missing person and not another scent. Even though A.J. was correct most of the time, I had a tendency to lose confidence if he headed in a direction that did not make sense to me. Like many other dog handlers, I sometimes found it hard to trust in my dog.

Stacey and I watched as Kea made a right turn down another road. After they disappeared, I allowed A.J. to resume his search. We ran past the intersection where Kea had made her turn. This meant the two search dogs were now working two different directions and only one dog could be correct. I secretly prayed that it was *my* dog that was on the correct scent trail. My hopes were dashed when moments later A.J. and I encountered a gate.

The gate was at least seven feet tall and was secured with a padlock that required a key. It was topped with razor wire and bordered by a rock formation on either side. Unless you had a key, there was no passing through this gate. I watched in disgust as A.J. sniffed the padlock, stuck his face through the small opening between the two chain link panels and wagged his tail. A.J. wanted to go through the gate.

"You idiot!" I hissed at A.J., "You missed the turn!"

I'm ashamed to say that I admonished my sweet bloodhound for doing what he was trained and born to do—he'd faithfully followed the scent I had asked him to follow. But like many dog handlers, I had jumped to the negative and assumed the worst. I assumed that Jeanne and Kea were on the correct scent trail and that A.J. was following the scent of an animal. I studied the narrow opening between the panels.

"Only a cat or small animal could pass through this gate," I said to Stacey.

I was ready to turn around and head back to the Command Post when, suddenly, Jeanne, Jason, and Kea came jogging up behind us. Moving out of the way, I watched as Kea tracked right up to the gate, sniffed the padlock, and stuck her face in between the panels just like A.J. had done. Suddenly, I began to regain some confidence in A.J. when I realized *both* the search-and-rescue dogs wanted to go through the same gate.

Jeanne radioed Command Post and learned that the residents of Paradise Park were issued keys to the padlock on the gate. I was skeptical. I thought it improbable that a man who had swallowed a bottle of sleeping pills and was intent on suicide would think clearly enough to grab his gun and remember to bring a key for a gate that was rarely used.

"A distraught man who just overdosed wouldn't go through a locked gate and then lock it behind him," I said to Jeanne. "Maybe I should go back and scent A.J. again."

Here was my dilemma. I knew that the search operation would likely shift in the direction that our search dogs tracked. If the missing man was not in fact on the other side of that gate, we could mistakenly lead the search efforts in the wrong direction. Sadly, at that time I was less concerned about the welfare of the missing man and more concerned about my reputation as a dog handler.

"Go ahead," Jeanne said, "But I'm waiting for the key." Jeanne trusted Kea. She had faith in her dog, something that eluded me at that moment. When I realized that Jeanne was going to wait at the gate for the key to arrive, I decided to wait with her.

After a short wait, the manager of the park arrived with the key. When he opened the gate, Kea and A.J. along with Jeanne, Jason, Stacey and I moved through to the other side. Both search dogs worked down the road—then Kea cut off to the right as A.J. cut off to the left. A.J. pulled Stacey and I into the belly of the forest, down a dirt path, and directly to the missing injured man who was lying face down.

"Search command, dog team one," Stacey radioed the command post. "We found the subject! Start an ambulance, code three!"

I administered first aid until the medical personnel arrived. Even though he had overdosed and shot himself, the man was still alive. As paramedics attended him, I turned around and knelt down in front of my hound.

"Good boooooy," I softly cooed. A.J. let out a soft moan of pleasure as I scratched the tender, pink insides of his floppy hound ears. I quietly praised my hound and reflected on the fact that my lack of faith in my dog had nearly cost this man his life. The irony is that later, A.J. and I flew to Chicago where we received the 1995 National Police Bloodhound Association's Lifesaving award for this case. The reality is that it was Jeanne's trust in Kea that saved that man's life. But because Kea was a golden retriever, not a bloodhound, she could not receive that award.

In addition to teaching me to trust A.J., God had used the suicidal man search to reinforce a critical spiritual principle. Through my fascinating journey, I've discovered that God is a faithful gatekeeper and there are no limits to the keys on His key ring. And even though a gate might be closed, padlocked, and topped with razor wire, it doesn't mean it's not the path that I'm supposed to follow.

Steven Spielberg once said, "It takes a visionary to stick with something that fails for many years." In my nineteen-year struggle to pioneer community-based pet detective services, I've encountered setback after setback; I've failed in so many ways. On several occasions during my journey, I've run into circumstances that appeared to be a locked gate, often taking me to the point where I wanted to give up. However, because of this search with A.J., I'm no longer so eager to turn around and head in a different direction. Instead I've learned to trust God, just like Jeanne trusted Kea, and to wait patiently for Him to meet me at my gate.

Additional Info

If You Have Lost a Pet

If you've lost a pet, there are highly effective lost pet recovery tips on Missing Pet Partnership's Web site at www.missingpetpartnership.org. In addition, MPP has a National Directory of Pet Detectives, some with dogs trained to find lost pets. MPP also has a Lost Pet Consultant program in which trained volunteers offer phone consultations to help educate, strategize with, and encourage pet owners who've lost a dog or a cat.

Pet Detective Training

If you're interested in being trained as a professional or volunteer pet detective, Kat offers Missing Animal Response webinar courses through her pet detective academy K-9 Pet Trackers, LLC. Kat has webinar courses that range from 6-weeks to 10-weeks in length. Her students include professional pet detectives, shelter workers, animal rescue volunteers, and other animal industry professionals. For more information on lost pet recovery training with Kat, visit www.katalbrecht.com/training.

K9 Pet Detective Training
For more information on how to evaluate and train a dog to find lost pets, check out Kat's book *Dog Detectives: Train Your Dog to Find Lost Pets* (http://tinyurl.com/nu4dfmr) and visit her K9 Training page at http://www.katalbrecht.com/K9train.php.

School / Library Visits
Kat speaks to middle grade and high school students on the secular topic of "Finding Your Life Purpose" with an emphasis on the exploration of hobbies, interests, and talents. If you're a teacher, librarian, or parent whom home-schools, visit www.igniteyourlifepurpose.org for school visit details.

Women's Ministries
Kat offers inspirational "Ignite Your Life Purpose" women's ministries and church youth group events, 3-day "Ignite Your Life Purpose" reflection retreats, and one-on-one life purpose coaching. If you've struggled to find purpose and passion in your life, come learn what the Bible says about life purpose and how you were woven by God for a specific purpose. To learn more about Kat's Life Purpose ministry, visit www.igniteyourlifepurpose.org.

Support Missing Pet Partnership
Missing Pet Partnership (MPP) offers lost pet coaching and has an amazing website that has helped recover thousands of lost pets. MPP is working to train staff and volunteers from animal shelters, rescue groups, and animal welfare organizations in the principles of lost pet recovery. MPP needs both volunteers and donor support. You can support our work by making a tax deductible donation through PayPal on our Web site at www.missingpetpartnership.org or by mailing a check to: Missing Pet Partnership, P.O. Box 3085, Federal Way, WA 98063.

Videos of Kat & Dogs

Video of Rachel as she searches for a missing cat named Manuel (search story featured in chapter 12):
http://tinyurl.com/pfmkcrt

Video of Kat and Becky Hiatt working Chase on a training trail followed by working Rachel on an actual search for a missing cat named Joseph:
http://tinyurl.com/lj6gf72

Video of A.J. as he searches for missing terrier Bubba (story featured in chapter 15): http://tinyurl.com/kntvppt

Video of Kat and Chase demonstrating a tracking training trail:
http://tinyurl.com/lz5kzt7

Video of Cheeto's work as a target cat:
http://tinyurl.com/ksa69pk

Video of Cheeto and Myron waving for dried salmon treats:
http://tinyurl.com/l35n2wx

Video of Kat giving instructions on how to capture a panicked dog:
http://tinyurl.com/ldksh4f

ACKNOWLEDGEMENTS

Thank you to the donors, volunteers, and board members who've supported Missing Pet Partnership and my vision to develop community-based lost pet services. I'm deeply grateful to both Jana Murphy and Bloomsbury USA for helping to create the first version of this book (*The Lost Pet Chronicles*). I'm especially grateful to digital rights director Annie Hwang and literary agent Jeff Kleinman from Folio Literary Management for making this new edition possible. Thanks to both Chris Schmidt for the lovely cover photo of Rachel and Karen Ashton for the cover artwork. I want to send a special thank you to my friend and pet detective graduate, Kimberly Freeman (www.lostcat-finder.com) for her copy edit work. Thank you to my best friend and husband Johnny for your unconditional love and support as we seek to grow together in God. And finally, I'd like to give all glory and praise to my Lord and Savior Jesus Christ for taking me on this incredible life journey simply because I was willing to believe and to obey.

AUTHOR BIO

Kat Albrecht is a police detective-turned-pet detective and the founder of Missing Pet Partnership (MPP), a national nonprofit organization dedicated to reuniting lost pets with their families and K9 Pet Trackers, LLC, the first-ever pet detective academy. Kat successfully pioneered the cross application of law enforcement investigative techniques and technologies to solve lost pet investigations. She is widely known as the leading authority on pet detective training. Since 1997, Kat has trained hundreds of professional pet detectives, volunteer pet detectives, animal control officers, veterinarians, and shelter staff in the analysis of human and animal behaviors that contribute to the homeless pet crisis. Kat and her search dogs (and target cats) have appeared on Animal Planet, and articles about her work have appeared in major publications like *People, Reader's Digest,* and *Parade.* Kat is the author of two books: *The Lost Pet Chronicles* (first published in 2004, revised and released in 2015 under the title *Pet Tracker*) and *Dog Detectives: Train Your Dog to Find Lost Pets.* Kat is an inspirational speaker who encourages teens (and adults) to find their own "life purpose." You can sign up for Kat's newsletter through her Web site at www.katalbrecht.com/contact.php, connect on LinkedIn at www.linkedin.com/in/katalbrecht, chat about her books on www.goodreads.com, follow her tweets at @katalbrecht, and like her Facebook page at www.facebook.com/katalbrechtpetdetective.

A.J. (left), Kat, and Chase (right)
Photo by UCSC Photography

24469159R00123

Printed in Great Britain
by Amazon